100 LANGUAGE GAMES

FOR AGES 0 TO 3

Easy-to-play games

Supporting first learning

Stages of development

CLARE BESWICK

CREDITS

British Library Cataloguing-in-Publication Data A catalogue record for this book is available from the British Library.

ISBN 0 439 98434 3

Author
Clare Beswick

Illustrations
Gaynor Berry

Editor
Lesley Sudlow

Assistant Editor
Saveria Mezzana

Series Designer
Anna Oliwa

Designer
Anna Oliwa

Designed using Adobe Pagemaker

Published by Scholastic Ltd,
Villiers House,
Clarendon Avenue,
Leamington Spa,
Warwickshire CV32 5PR

Visit our website at www.scholastic.co.uk
Printed by Belmont Press
1 2 3 4 5 6 7 8 9 0   3 4 5 6 7 8 9 0 1 2

Acknowledgements

The publishers gratefully acknowledge permission to reproduce the following copyright material:

© **Corbis:** p6, p8, p68, p76, p82, p100

© **Digital Stock:** cover, p5, p67, p82

© **Digital Vision Ltd:** p52

© **Ingram Publishing:** cover, p1, p3, p12, p19, p20, p25, p30, p33, p35, p43, p54, p56, p61, p84, p91, p107, 118, 123

© **Photodisc:** p4, p34, p75, p78, p108

© **John Fortunato/SODA:** p68, p109, p123

© **Dan Howell/SODA:** p7, p23, p35, p56, p69, p111

© **Ken Karp/SODA:** p54, p96

© **James Levin/SODA:** p38, p49, p112

© **Dan Powell/SODA:** p9, p10, p24, p28, p37, p51, p52, p53, p81, p96, p112, p114

© **Clara Von Aich/SODA:** p62

© **Photodisc via SODA:** p38, p40, p66, p73, p95

© **Stockbyte:** cover, p1, p3, p4, p16, p20, p45, p49, p56, p59, p61, p89, p93, p97, p115, p118, p121

© **William Gray:** p13, p17, p19, p32, p34, p43, p48, p59, p63, p71, p79, p85, p90, p92, p99, p101, p106, p118

J B Cramer & Co Ltd for two verses of 'I Love to Row in My Big Blue Boat' from *Playtime Tunes for Nursery School* by Marion Anderson © 1969, Marion Anderson (1969, J B Cramer & Co Ltd)

Every effort has been made to trace copyright holders and the publishers apologise for any inadvertent omissions.

CONTENTS

CHAPTER 1

READY, STEADY, GO

CHAPTER 2

TAKING TURNS

CHAPTER 3

LET'S PRETEND

CHAPTER 4

LIVELY TIMES

CONTENTS

CHAPTER 5

OUT AND ABOUT

CHAPTER 6

FRIENDS TOGETHER

CHAPTER 7

BUSY WITH BOOKS

CHAPTER 8

JUST THE TWO OF US

INTRODUCTION

From the very beginning

Even before your baby was born, he could hear your voice and those of family and friends around you. He could sense the rhythm of your world – if you were busy or resting. Unborn babies can hear the sounds around them, and they respond to familiar and new noises differently. From the moment of birth, your baby is starting to learn language. Even new-born babies are aware of sounds around them. They listen to the speech of those who are caring for them. They startle or cry if they hear an unexpected noise, and they are still when they hear your voice and other familiar and pleasurable sounds.

New-born babies are setting off on the path through our social world towards being effective communicators. They will learn to understand and use speech and body language, and will communicate effectively with others, understanding the social rules that smooth the flow of conversation and communication.

More than words

Language is so much more than the words and phrases that we use every day to communicate. It is about communicating without words, perhaps by looking at another person as you speak to and listen to them, as well as glances and stares. Language means using and understanding facial expressions, for example, the smile, frown or cynical roll of the eyes. It is about understanding and using gestures, from the simple 'goodbye' wave to the more complex expressive use of hands to add emphasis as we talk. By using the pointing gesture, we can point to show another person what we want or need, show a person something of interest or give a direction. Children need to learn how to understand and use all of this.

Language is about timing, such as taking turns in conversation. It is also about listening, on a one-to-one basis or as part of a group, about staying focused and about sharing our attention with another person. When we talk to someone, we have a shared interest in the conversation, are sensitive to the needs and interests of the other person, and read the signals if they are getting bored. All these skills need to be brought together with the development of speech to enable babies and children to gradually develop into articulate thinking individuals and active listeners.

Learning language

Every baby is unique, and although we can generalise about the way in which babies and young children develop language, the pace at which each baby and child develops varies markedly. These differences are completely natural and part of what makes your baby an individual. It is important to remember that the pace at which your baby and young child gains these early language skills is not an indicator of their overall potential but the moment on a stepping-stone on the path towards language. All babies develop at their own paces. They often develop more quickly in some areas of their development, perhaps in their physical skills and movement, and less quickly in other areas. If you do have any concerns about any part of your child's development, you should contact your health visitor or family doctor.

Babies and young children generally develop language step by step along a fairly clear route. Babies develop certain skills before words; they are known as preverbal skills and are the building blocks of communication.

These include skills such as looking and listening, pointing and other gestures, understanding turn-taking and anticipating events, such as during a game of 'Ready, steady, go'. When they have a range of preverbal skills, babies and young children begin to recognise familiar objects in their world and start to understand what they are used for, such as recognising the spoon and knowing that it carries food to their mouth. Gradually, they link the words that label these objects to the actual objects. They know that when you say 'spoon', it means the object that brings food. The number of first words that they understand grows. Soon, your child will begin to experiment with imitating words and sounds. This is his way of using some first words to let you know what he wants.

Understanding language

Your child's understanding grows gradually, so that around the age of two and a half, he can often understand phrases with two or three information-carrying key words. Children will understand more than they can say, but once they can understand two- and three-word phrases, they will start putting words together. This builds quickly and soon most children will be using sentences with words to label objects, words to describe actions and also words to indicate possession, for example, 'Mummy's keys'. They will start to use words to describe the size and colour of objects and also their position, such as 'in', 'on' or 'under'.

At first, your child will talk mostly about the things that interest him in his immediate world, essentially what he wants or needs. This develops gradually so that he can use speech for lots of different purposes. He will learn to tell you about past events, about the future, and to reason with you. He will begin to wonder how things work and ask why, and he will use this to ask you endless questions.

Routines and play

The everyday tasks of caring for your baby offer plenty of opportunity to help early language development. Take the time, when you are changing nappies, bathing, dressing or feeding, to focus on his emerging language and communication skills, for example:

- sing and talk to your baby, emphasising familiar phrases
- tell your baby what you are doing
- get on the same level as your baby, so you can look into each other's faces
- really listen to your baby and try to understand his world from his point of view.

For older babies and young children, you can also:

- let your child help you with everyday tasks
- listen to your child and take the time to enjoy his attempts at communication
- show your child that you are pleased
- use your child's name to gain his attention, before speaking to him
- speak with a clear and animated voice – be yourself as well as being fun.

Listening to your baby and young child

Listening is a skill that needs to be learned and practised. Your baby needs to learn to attend to voices and listen carefully to all that is going on around him. Older babies and children are constantly developing their listening skills, learning to concentrate on the important things and to maintain their attention.

As a parent or carer, you need to learn to listen to your baby and tune into your child. Try to make some uninterrupted time every day for you and your child to get to know each other. Spend a couple of minutes relaxing together while you watch your child, listening carefully to the range of sounds that he is making and thinking about how he is communicating with you and others.

Playing together

Babies and young children are naturally curious and love to explore. They learn best through play, with plenty of uninterrupted time to discover their world. Your child needs you to be available to help him in his play, keep him safe and provide interesting opportunities, but most of all, to be available to celebrate and wonder at his discoveries.

You are your baby's favourite toy thing and you can provide endless entertainment. Babies and young children need lots of attention, but also the freedom and time to play and explore independently. They need a balance of time to:

- explore independently
- play purposefully with an adult
- play alongside an adult
- help you and be with you as you go about daily life
- share songs, books and rhymes
- relax with you and enjoy quiet, restful play.

Using the games

The games in this book are designed for purposeful play with an adult. They are organised so that you can dip into different chapters and fit them around your child's routine. Try to match them to your child's current interests and enthusiasms. You do not need to work through the games in any particular order. For ease, they are arranged into three different stages: 'Before words', 'First words' and 'Putting words together'.

Each game takes only a few minutes. All the games aim to encourage the development of early language skills and help to move your baby and young child in a fun and engaging way towards effective communication. Play should always be fun and enjoyable, both to you and your child. Remain flexible – if your baby is enjoying playing the game in a different way, then let him take the lead and play alongside him.

Before you play the games, read each one carefully and gather together everything you need. Switch off the television and remove as many distractions as possible. Be calm and relaxed, and sit so that your face and your child's are on the same level. Enjoy the game but always try to move on from it before your child loses interest. It is always easier to come back to a game if you have decided that the game is finished than if your child has.

CHAPTER 1

From the very moment that a baby is born, she is a unique individual and is already learning and practising the skills that she needs to develop to become an effective communicator. Within the first few months of her life, she is able to let you know how she feels and what she wants. Before babies develop first words, they learn to use a range of skills that are the building blocks of language skills. The way that you respond to your baby at this stage is very important and influences the way in which she develops language. The games in this chapter focus on using a sense of anticipation to have fun together while making a great start with language.

READY, STEADY, GO

THE FIRST SIX MONTHS

Since birth, your baby has been aware of sounds. She has been listening to the voices of those close to her and heard sounds all around her. You may have noticed that your baby startled or cried if she heard an unexpected sound. She may have stilled to new sounds. By three months, your baby is already on the way to becoming an effective communicator. She will turn to you when you speak, and smile when she hears your voice. Between four and six months, many babies become responsive to changes in the tone of your voice and become fascinated by toys that make sounds and music.

How you can help

- Talk to your baby as much as possible, particularly during dressing, feeding and changing times.
- Sing to your baby.
- Spend time playing with your baby, face to face, tuning into her facial expressions and sounds.

DEVELOPING UNDERSTANDING

From seven to twelve months is an exciting time in your baby's life. He listens when you speak to him, and turns to look at your face when you call his name. He develops first understanding and is beginning to have a sense of anticipation that something is going to happen. Understanding and sharing a sense of anticipation is an important step in the 'before words' stage of language development. Your baby will love to play 'Peek-a-boo' and other games where exciting things follow a pause, such as 'Ready, steady, go'.

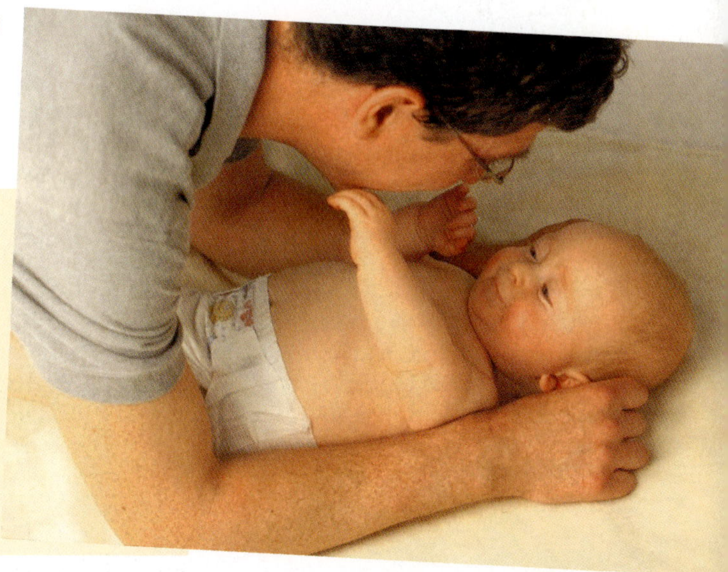

How you can help

- Tell your baby what you are going to do for him next. Sprinkle some water on his toes and fingers and say, 'It's bathtime, here it comes – in the bath' as you lower him into the water.
- Mealtimes are a great time to build anticipation. When his meal is almost ready, say to your baby, 'Its coming' and sometimes build the drama, for example, 'Dinner's coming, coming,

coming – here it is!' as you bring the bowl to the tray.

- Take every opportunity to have fun play by anticipating the next event or action. Babies rarely tire of playing 'Ready, steady, go' or 'It's coming'.

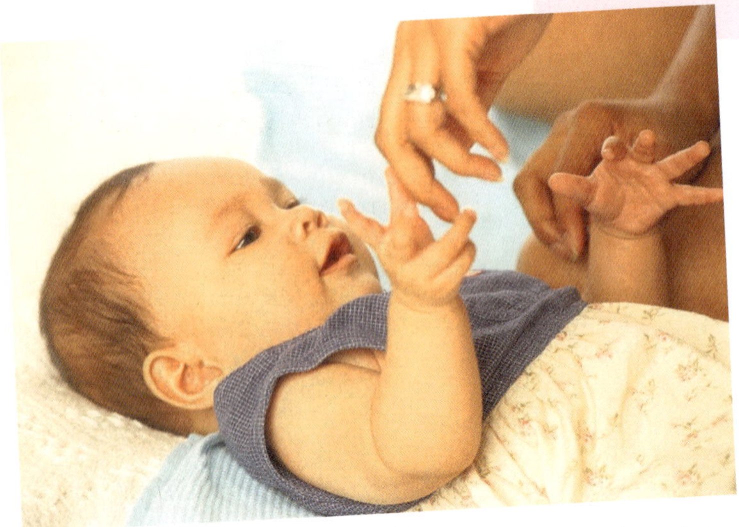

- Building towers will be a favourite with your child. Use an exaggerated gasp just before you or your child knocks down the tower. Build the tower, then whisper, 'Ready, steady...', give an exaggerated gasp, then say, 'Go!' as you knock down the tower.

BABY TALK

Around the end of your baby's first year, she will begin to develop pointing to objects, firstly to things that she wants, for example, her cup or favourite toy, then later to things that she wants you to see, perhaps a bus coming or plane high in the sky. It is around this time that you may notice that your baby recognises the name of familiar objects and is beginning to respond to simple requests such as, 'Where's Teddy?'.

Older babies and toddlers will babble with you conversationally, taking turns and indulging in some baby-talk exchanges. The sense of anticipation and understanding as your child moves towards her first words will help her to time them and make her words have great meaning and effect.

How you can help

- Talk to your baby as you go about your daily life, chatting about what you are doing.
- Make time every day for uninterrupted talk with your child. Sit so that you can gaze at each other's faces. Enjoy making faces and funny noises, sing quietly to your baby and respond to her sounds with pleasure, imitating them and taking turns to make the sounds.
- Listen intently to your baby and gaze with smiles into her face when she babbles to you. Get down to your baby's eye level when she talks to you and smile at her with encouragement.
- Indulge in some baby talk, echoing babble sound back to your child conversationally. Show her that you are pleased to hear her and are enjoying the chat.

BUILDING WORDS

During his second year, your baby will continue to use pointing, but soon he may start to use a few words to label objects, then later on be able to point to a few body parts. His understanding of language and his world will grow quickly. By their third year, most young children will be understanding and will be using two- and three-word phrases. Many will enjoy simple turn-taking conversation.

How you can help

- Play lots of 'Ready, steady, go' games giving your child the opportunity to say, 'Go!' to make the action happen – the more dramatic the action, the better.
- Turn off the television or radio so that your child can concentrate without distraction.
- Action rhymes and finger rhymes are a good opportunity for you to share special one-to-one times. Pause in the middle of a favourite rhyme, be aware of your child's anticipation, and encourage him to say, 'Go!' or 'More' for you to continue the rhyme.
- Play tickle games such as 'Round and round the garden like a teddy bear'. These are important in developing your child's anticipation and first words.

READY, STEADY, GO

STAGE
Before words

LEARNING OPPORTUNITIES
- To develop a sense of anticipation
- To encourage reaching and an understanding of the outstretched gesture 'Give it to me'.

YOU WILL NEED
A chiffon scarf or other silky fabric square.

Blow wind blow

Sharing the game

- Sit opposite your baby so that your faces are at the same level.
- Blow the chiffon scarf gently towards your baby, then give it to him to explore.
- Stroke his cheek gently with the scarf and run it through his fingers. Hold it up so that he can see your face through the scarf, then blow it gently across the room.
- Return the scarf to your baby and after he has had a little time to play with it, stretch out your hand towards him, palm upwards, and ask him to give you the scarf by saying, 'Give me the scarf, please'. Help your baby to give you the scarf.
- If your baby does not want to let go of the scarf, gently stroke the back of his hand, repeating your request and your baby will release the scarf.

- Hold the scarf in front of you and call your baby's name to gain his attention. Gently blow the scarf towards him, but make sure that it does not go over his face. Help your baby to reach for the scarf, feel it and give it back to you.
- Encourage your baby to anticipate the release of the scarf by calling his name, then say, 'Ready, steady...', and pause before saying, 'Go!' and blowing the scarf.
- Repeat the game often, encouraging your baby to be an active participant in it, peeking through the scarf at your face, stretching for the scarf and enjoying the silky feel and the surprise as it floats across the room.

Taking it further

- Offer your baby the choice of two scarves to give to you to play the game with.
- Blow the scarf high into the air and let it fall gently down on your baby's toys or tray.

READY, STEADY, GO

STAGE
Before words

LEARNING OPPORTUNITIES
- To give eye contact and smiles
- To ask for 'more' with a glance or sound.

YOU WILL NEED
Two hats.

Nod, nod, nod

Sharing the game

- Sit opposite your baby so that your faces are at the same level.
- Give a hat to your baby to explore.
- Hold out an outstretched hand for your baby to give you the hat. Take it gently and say, 'Thank you'.
- Put the hat on your head making eye contact with your baby. Make a funny face, then suddenly drop your head forwards so that the hat falls into your lap. Smile and laugh with your baby.
- Ask your baby, 'Again?'. Wait for a glance, smile or sound and accept this as a request for you to do it again. Repeat while you are both enjoying the game.
- Offer your baby a choice of two hats. Help her to pick up and pass you the hat that she wants you to use for the game by saying, 'This one?' while pointing to one of them.
- Use a lively happy voice and be sure to give your baby time to respond before you prompt her by modelling what you want her to do next.
- End the game with smiles, praise and a cuddle.

Taking it further

- Put the hat in a shoebox next to your baby and wait for her to pass it to you before repeating the game.
- Gently put the hat on your baby's head, then tip it off and say, 'Boo!' as it falls down.
- Offer the hat to your baby and help her to put it on your head, then repeat the game.

READY, STEADY, GO

STAGE
Before words

LEARNING OPPORTUNITIES
- To understand surprise
- To understand that an object still exists even though it is out of sight.

YOU WILL NEED
A teddy; blanket.

Where's Teddy?

Sharing the game

- Sit opposite your baby so that your faces are at the same level.
- Give the teddy a hug and say, 'Ah, hug Teddy'.
- Pass the teddy to your baby and let him explore it. Help him to give the teddy a hug while you say, 'Ah, hug Teddy'.
- Gently put the teddy on the floor and cover it with the blanket. Let your baby see you covering the teddy.
- Call your baby's name, then, using a surprised voice, ask, 'Where's Teddy?'. Help your baby to pull the blanket from the teddy and say excitedly, 'Look, here's Teddy!'. Pick the teddy up and give it a hug.
- Give the teddy to your baby to hug, then cover it up again and repeat the game.

- Allow your baby plenty of time to respond and to explore the teddy and the blanket.
- Use the same language and simple gestures each time you play, for example, hug the teddy and say, 'Ah, hug Teddy' or say to your baby, 'Give Teddy a hug', while stretching out your hand.
- Try covering the teddy with a blanket, while your baby is holding the teddy. Give your baby time to actually feel and hug the teddy although he is unable to see it. Ask your baby, 'Where's Teddy?'. Pull the blanket off gently, while he is still holding the teddy.

Taking it further

- Help your baby to put the blanket over the teddy and pull it off when you ask, 'Where's Teddy?'.
- Try playing the game with a dolly or other familiar toys.
- Play the game while you are dressing your baby, by hiding his socks under the cover.

READY, STEADY, GO

STAGE
Before words

LEARNING OPPORTUNITIES
- To ask for 'more' by making a sound
- To make a choice by looking or pointing.

YOU WILL NEED
A doll and teddy or other soft toys; sofa or chair.

Look out, Dolly!

Sharing the game

- Sit opposite your baby on the floor so that your faces are at the same level, close to a sofa or chair.
- Pick up the doll and give it to your baby to explore. Say to her, 'Look, it's Dolly'.
- After your baby has had an opportunity to explore the doll, ask for it back by calling your baby's name to get her attention. Say, 'Dolly, please' with an outstretched hand. If your baby does not look at you when you call her name, wait for a moment until she pauses in her play, then call her name again, this time gently touching her cheek as you do so. This will help to gain her attention.
- Walk the doll along the sofa or chair, singing, 'This is the way that Dolly walks, Dolly walks, Dolly walks'. As you reach the edge of the sofa, pause and say, 'Oh no, look out, Dolly!', then let the doll fall off the sofa dramatically. Pick the doll up, hug her and say, 'Ah, Dolly's all right'. Then ask your baby, 'Again?'.

- Make the doll's antic fun and spectacular to your baby. Encourage her to look or make a sound when you ask, 'Again?'. If she does glance at the dolly, or vocalise, accept this as intending to mean 'Yes, do it again', and praise your baby.
- Be animated and involved, and your baby will respond to the sense of fun and shared attention on the game.
- Offer your baby a choice of doll or teddy. If she makes a choice by looking, gently take her hand towards her choice and, with your hand, show her a pointing gesture. Say, 'This one?', then repeat the game with her choice of toy.

Taking it further

- Play the same game, but this time let the doll slide down the cushions on the sofa.
- Start the game with 'Ready, steady, go' to build up the anticipation. Give your baby the opportunity to say, 'Go!' to start the game.

STAGE
First words

LEARNING OPPORTUNITIES
- To ask for 'more'
- To use word and gesture for 'gone'.

YOU WILL NEED
A pot of bubbles; bubble wand.

Bubble fun

Sharing the game

- Sit on the floor opposite your baby so that your faces are at the same level.
- Hold the bubbles between you and call your baby's name gently to gain his attention.
- Say, 'Look, bubbles!' and blow a few bubbles into the air between you. As your baby reaches for the bubbles, say, 'Pop!' as he catches each bubble. Raise your hands, palms upwards, to make a 'gone' gesture and say, 'Gone!' when all the bubbles have disappeared.
- Wait for a moment until your baby reaches for the bubble pot, then ask, 'More?'. If he reaches for the pot, show him a pointing gesture and repeat, 'More?', then reward him with more bubbles.
- Play the game often, each time encouraging your child to request more and helping him to understand and copy the word 'Gone!' and the gesture for it.

Taking it further

- Play the game outside on a soft surface. The breeze will blow the bubbles away from your baby and encourage him to move about.
- Make this game part of your baby's bathtime play, too.
- Create larger bubbles by filling a bowl with a mixture of water and washing-up liquid. Dip a funnel or an old tennis racket in the mixture and wave it gently in the air to release the bubbles.
- Play the 'Asking for more and gesturing "gone"' game at drink time, too, or perhaps when your child is having a favourite snack.

STAGE
First words

LEARNING OPPORTUNITIES
- To imitate use of familiar objects
- To encourage first words.

YOU WILL NEED
Stretchy material or Lycra fabric; your child's cup, brush and flannel.

Pull, pull, pull

Sharing the game

- Sit on the floor with your child and help her to grasp the edge of the fabric. Holding the other side of the fabric, gently stretch it between you. When it is taut say, 'Ready, steady...', then pause and say, 'Go!'. Let go of the fabric so that it pings back together.
- Repeat this, encouraging your child to say, 'Go!' so that she directs the release of the fabric herself.
- Play this often so that your child can enjoy the excitement of the game.
- After some time, gently hide your child's brush under the stretched fabric. Repeat the game and appear surprised when the brush is found under the fabric. Pick up the brush and pretend to brush your hair. Hand the brush to your child and help her to brush her hair.
- As your child pretends to use the brush, sing, 'This is the way we brush our hair, brush our hair, brush our hair' to the tune of 'Here We Go Round the Mulberry Bush' (Traditional).
- Repeat the game with a cup. When your child discovers the cup, help her to imitate having a drink, then sing, 'This is the way we have a drink, have a drink, have a drink'.
- Play again, this time with the flannel, singing, 'This is the way we wash our face, wash our face, wash our face'.

Taking it further

- Put your child's cup, brush and flannel in a box and let her choose and place one of the objects under the cloth, before beginning the stretching game.
- Add different everyday objects such as a spoon, shoe or book.

READY, STEADY, GO

STAGE
First words

LEARNING OPPORTUNITIES
- To recognise words for body parts
- To point to own body parts and on someone else.

YOU WILL NEED
A comfortable chair or area; doll or teddy.

Coming to tickle

Sharing the game

- Find a chair or an area to sit comfortably with your child. Play 'Peek-a-boo' gently, or another favourite game, to relax.
- Quietly call your child's name. When you have his attention, say his name then say, 'I'm coming to tickle your...'. Pause, give an exaggerated gasp sound, then say, 'Hands!' and tickle his hands for a moment, laughing with him.
- If your child has enjoyed the game, play again. After a couple of repetitions, ask, 'Should we tickle your...?'. Wait for him to offer a body part or say a word. If he holds out a foot, or lifts his jumper to be tickled, name the body part and play again. Say, 'I'm coming to tickle your...'. Pause for your child to attempt the word 'toes'.
- The pause and exaggerated gasp is important as it gives your child a clear signal that this is his chance to take control of the game, by offering a body part or saying a word himself.
- When your child understands the game and is able to point to three of his own body parts, introduce the doll (or teddy) to the game. Say, 'Let's tickle Dolly'. Ask your child, 'Should we tickle Dolly's tummy or her ears?'.

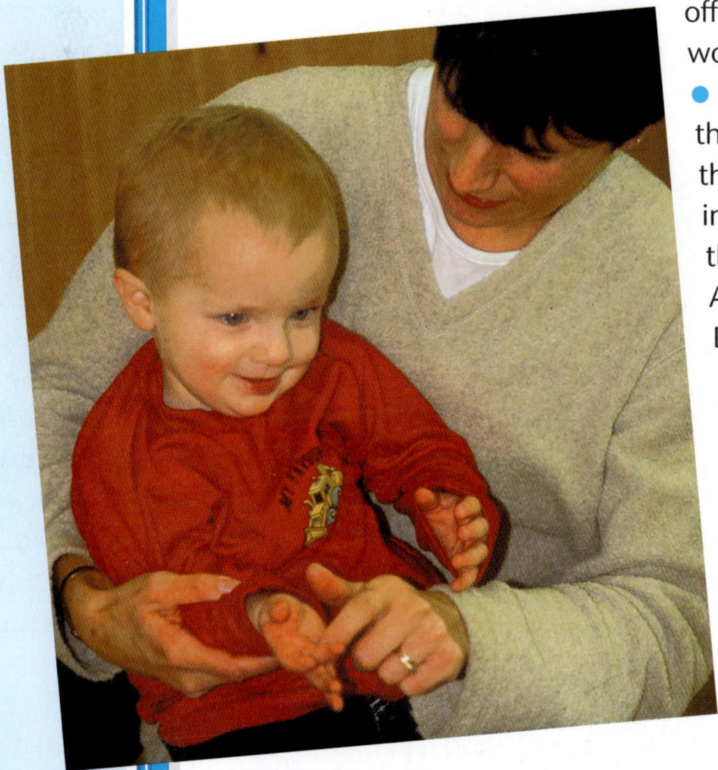

Taking it further

- Play the game spontaneously from a distance as you go about your daily routine. Call across the room to your child, then say, 'I'm coming to tickle your... toes!' and wait for him to lift his toes up, ready to enjoy the game.
- Be sensitive to your child's mood and play gentle tickle games when he is happy and relaxed. Keep this sort of play to short bursts and always stop the game before your child becomes tired.

READY, STEADY, GO

STAGE
First words

LEARNING OPPORTUNITIES
- To enjoy rhymes
- To make a choice.

YOU WILL NEED
A large cardboard box; cushion (optional).

In the box

Sharing the game

- Place the cardboard box on the floor and help your child to explore it. Add a cushion, if necessary, and encourage your child to sit in the box. Kneel on the floor, facing her.
- Gently tip the box from side to side and make up a simple tune as you sing to your child:

  All aboard, all aboard the boat.
  Here we go side to side, and
  Side to side and side to side, again.
- Pause and ask your child if she would like to play again. Encourage her to copy the word 'again' and say, 'Do you want the boat song?' emphasising the word 'boat'. Repeat the song and actions.

- Introduce a second song and an up-and-down action. Gently bump the box up and down at the front singing, to a simple tune:

  On the horse, climb on the horse
  Here we go jiggety jog, and
  Jiggety jog and jiggety jog, again.
- Repeat the songs and games. Each time, ask your child to choose a game. If she moves the box from side to side, say, 'Do you want the boat?'. Pause to give her a chance to imitate the word 'boat' and then sing the song.
- Make sure to end the game while your child is still having fun, so that she will be happy to play again another day.

Taking it further

- When your child is sat in the cardboard box, offer her a choice of two soft toys to take with her on her ride.
- Pause in the middle of the song, so that your child has to ask you to continue with a word or a gesture.

STAGE
Putting words together

LEARNING OPPORTUNITIES
- To encourage use of object and action word together
- To listen to and use two words together.

YOU WILL NEED
Several small boxes; familiar objects such as a cup, spoon, brush, shoe, car, ball, small teddy, doll, book, keys and so on.

Finding fun

Sharing the game

- Encourage your child to explore the empty boxes.
- Gather the boxes together and place three familiar objects in each box. Give each box a shake to make it more interesting to your child, then place it down on the floor.
- Invite your child to choose which box to explore first. As he opens the box, ask him to find two of the objects. Give your child plenty of time to respond. Prompt him if necessary by repeating the request and stressing the name of the object that he is still to find. Praise your child for listening well.
- Continue playing the game, varying the objects and swapping the boxes around.
- Later, place the doll or teddy in one of the boxes, with two of the familiar objects. When your child opens the box, pick up the items and choose one of the familiar objects and use it with the doll or teddy. For example, pretend to give Teddy a drink. Ask your child, 'What is Teddy doing?'. Encourage him to respond with 'Teddy drinking'. If he says the object words, for example, 'cup tea', gently encourage him by modelling the correct phrase.

Taking it further

- Help your child to match each of the objects from the box with another object from around the house.
- Play a bathtime game of hiding objects under the flannel or some bubbles and asking your child to find two objects out of a choice of up to six items.

READY, STEADY, GO

STAGE
Putting words together

LEARNING OPPORTUNITIES
- To encourage two-word phrases
- To use common adjectives, such as for size or colour.

YOU WILL NEED
A cardboard tube; selection of small toys and familiar objects that are small enough to roll down the tube, for example, a car, ball and spoon.

Surprise time

Sharing the game

- Sit with your child on the floor and give her the cardboard tube to explore. Encourage her to peek through it, blow down it and drop toys through it.
- Hold the cardboard tube at an angle so that when you post the toys through they will fall close to your child. Gain your child's attention by calling her name, then say, 'Ready, steady...', and pause before saying, 'Go!', then post the toy through the tube.
- Ask your child, 'What have you got?' and prompt her, if necessary, with, 'Look, it's a...', then pause for her to say what she has found. If she uses one word, for example, 'car', respond with, 'Look, red car'.
- Encourage your child to use two and three words together so that she not only names the actual object but also tells you something about it, such as its colour or size, or perhaps to whom it belongs, for example, 'Mummy's keys'.
- Listen to the phrases that your child uses, and model phrases for her that include object and action words, such as 'Baby crying', or two-word phrases that include possession, such as 'Teddy's hat'.

Taking it further

- Take it in turns with your child to post the objects down the tube.
- Ask your child to post an object down the tube when you describe it by its use, for example, 'Find something that opens doors' (keys), or perhaps ask her to find an object of a particular colour, for example, 'Find me something blue'.

READY, STEADY, GO

STAGE
Putting words together

LEARNING OPPORTUNITIES
- To be familiar with animal sounds and names
- To listen and carry out two requests.

YOU WILL NEED
Toy farm animals including cows, sheep, pigs, ducks and dog; shoebox; cloth; felt-tipped pens.

Who is in the shed?

Sharing the game

- Stand the open shoebox on its side to make a shed for the farm animals. Use the felt-tipped pens to draw a few blades of grass on to the lid to create a field next to the shed.
- Encourage your child to cover his eyes with his hands while you place some cows in the shed and sheep in the field. Cover the scene with the cloth.
- Invite your child to open his eyes and ask him to guess who is in the field and who is in the shed, as you sing this song, to the tune of 'Old Macdonald Had a Farm' (Traditional) and make the sounds:

  Old Macdonald had a farm, E-I-E-I-O!
  And in the field there was a baa,
  baa, baa, baa, baa, baa.
  And in the shed there was a moo,
  moo, moo, moo, moo, moo.

- Help your child to wait until the end of the song and then tell you which animals are in the field and which are in the shed. Lift the cloth together to see if he is correct.
- Repeat the game, taking it in turns with your child to place the animals in the field or in the shed.
- Later, close your eyes and ask your child to put the pigs in the shed and the dog in the field. When he is ready, you can sing the song for him while he checks out if he has done it correctly.
- Vary the game by changing the field for a pond, sitting the ducks on the roof of the shed and standing the pigs in the pond.

Taking it further

- Practise counting to three with your child, by helping him to count the animals that are in the field, or by asking him to put, for example, two ducks in the shed and one cow in the field.

READY, STEADY, GO

STAGE
Putting words together

LEARNING OPPORTUNITIES
- To understand 'in', 'on' and 'under'
- To use descriptive words such as 'big' and 'little', 'fast' and 'slow'.

YOU WILL NEED
Big and small cars or lorries; two trays or pieces of thick card to make a bridge and a hill; box to create a garage.

Traffic-lights

Sharing the game

- Help your child to build a bridge and a hill for the vehicles and set the box on its side to create a garage.
- Invite your child to choose a car or lorry. Play alongside her, describing to her where the vehicles are going, emphasising the positional words, for example, '*on* the bridge', '*under* the bridge', '*down* the hill' and so on.
- When you call out, 'Red!', all the cars must stop. Describe where your car is, for example, at the bottom of the hill, then ask your child to tell you where her car is, for example, under the bridge. Call out, 'Green!' for the cars to set off again. Resume your commentary, stressing key words that describe position.
- When you shout, 'Yellow!', all the cars must stop and your child must close her eyes while you position her car on the track. Ask her to open her eyes and to find her car, then invite her to tell you where it is positioned, before setting off again.
- Continue the game with different vehicles, introducing 'big' and 'little' in your commentary, but keeping the traffic-light rules the same. Stop often to give your child a chance to use descriptive words. Encourage her to use positional words as well as words describing size.

Taking it further

- Play the traffic-light game with your child in the park or in your garden, using yourselves as the vehicles, climbing in, on and under different things, and stopping for the red light to describe where you are, before moving on for the green light.

CHAPTER 2

The understanding of language starts with an appreciation of familiar objects, actions and gestures. The games in this chapter use turn-taking as a way of helping babies and young children to build a sound perception of language – the foundation of effective communication. From the first days of their lives, babies are fascinated by other people. Your baby will want to be part of your world as well as interact with others. He will need to recognise familiar objects and what they are used for, understand gestures, and build and enjoy communication with familiar people before knowing and using words and phrases.

TAKING TURNS

EVERYDAY SITUATIONS

An early stage in developing understanding is recognising familiar situations and routines. Your baby will use the clues that are part of regular routines in her life to help her begin to make sense of her world. She will use all her senses to become familiar with, and to tune into, events in her life. Your baby will know that being undressed and hugged in a warm towel means that it is almost bathtime, or that perhaps the sound of your feet outside her room means that soon you will be lifting her out of her cot.

How you can help

- Be consistent in the way that you care for your baby's physical needs, for example, keep the routine the same, sing to her and play the same tickle and touch games.
- Use simple and familiar words to talk to your baby about what is happening.
- Give your baby an indication about what is going to happen, for example, when you are going out, let her feel the door key, and say, 'Time to go out', or give your baby a spoon to hold while you prepare her meal.
- Sing songs and rhymes to your baby.
- Share picture and fabric books with your baby. Have a selection of touch-and-feel books where she can feel as well as see the pictures.

FAMILIAR OBJECTS AND PICTURES

Babies and young children rely heavily on gesture and other signs to help them make sense of the world. Gestures such as the outstretched hand are quickly interpreted as meaning 'they want me to give them

something'. Babies also learn to use gestures such as waving 'goodbye'. The understanding of the idea and gesture for 'all gone' is a great motivator for learning to make sounds to ask for 'more'. Pointing is another very effective gesture for older babies and young children as it is an ideal way of getting what they want.

As your baby's understanding of gestures and familiar routines is growing, he will also begin to recognise objects that are used frequently in his world, for example, he will begin to understand what you mean when you say, 'cup', 'shoe', 'sock', 'ball' and 'car'. He will learn that these familiar objects have a use and he will want to try them out.

Later, your young child will recognise photographs and simple pictures of these objects, and gradually his understanding will grow.

How you can help

- Speak clearly to your child. Use familiar words and give him plenty of time to explore new objects.
- Use gestures and words in the correct context. Encourage your baby to imitate gestures and actions, such as waving 'goodbye' or clapping hands.
- When you are talking to your child, attract his attention by saying his name first, so that he knows that you are talking directly to him.
- Show your child what objects are used for. For example, if he is holding a brush, pretend to brush his hair with it, then pretend to brush your hair.
- Spend time looking at picture books with your child. Sing songs and rhymes all the time, not just at bedtime.

UNDERSTANDING WORDS AND PHRASES

As your child learns to recognise more and more objects, she will begin to understand single words. She will know what you mean when you name different objects and will be able to point to objects as well as to some body parts. As this understanding of single words grows, your child will also learn to identify pictures of familiar words. She will be able to point to pictures in a book – for example, when you say 'Show me the car', she will point to the picture of the car. First, she will recognise photographs of familiar objects, but she will soon learn that pictures and line drawings also represent the same familiar objects.

Before long, your child will begin to recognise action words and understand crying, sleeping, jumping, running and many more. Next will come her understanding of two words together in a phrase. She will soon be able to point to Mummy's bag from a selection of bags and will be able to choose objects from a group. For example, if you ask your child, 'Where's the ball and the book?', she will be able to understand the two key words, 'ball' and 'book'.

From this landmark stage, understanding of language flourishes and soon your child will be understanding longer phrases, as well as complex sentences with words that show possession, for example, 'Dog's bone', or attributes such as colour and size. She will also begin to develop understanding of words that describe position such as 'in', 'on' and 'under'.

How you can help

- Look at books with clear pictures and photographs with your child.
- Enjoy sharing music, action rhymes and simple games with your child.
- Listen carefully to your child and model clearly words that she finds difficult.
- Go down to your child's level when you are talking to her.
- Think about your child's understanding of language and keep your requests and instructions short and simple.
- Enjoy your child's emerging language – it is a precious gift.

TAKING TURNS

STAGE
Before words

LEARNING OPPORTUNITY
- To imitate actions and gestures.

YOU WILL NEED
A small balloon.

THINK FIRST! Remember to put the balloon well out of reach of your baby. Babies and young children should never be left alone to play with balloons – a burst balloon is a choking hazard.

Balloon delight

Sharing the game

- Sit opposite your baby on the floor, with your faces at the same level.
- Hold the balloon gently in front of you and pat it up and down for your baby to watch while you sing, 'Up and down, up and down'.
- Support the balloon on the floor and pat it. Help your baby to copy you while you sing, 'Pat the balloon, pat the balloon, pat, pat, pat'.
- Pass the balloon to your baby and sing the patting song for him. Join in with him as he pats the balloon.
- Stretch out your hand and ask your child to give the balloon back to you.
- Repeat the 'Up and down' game, then gently pat the balloon towards your baby. Use an outstretched hand gesture to make your baby understand that he must return it to you.
- Help your baby to pat the balloon back and forth between you.
- Next, hold the balloon in front of your face and play 'Peek-a-boo' with your baby. If he enjoys this game, hold the balloon close to his face and say, 'Peek-a...', then move the balloon away so that he can see you and say, 'Boo!'.
- Give your baby lots of smiles and encouragement. End the game before he becomes distracted.

Taking it further

- Hide the balloon behind your back. Ask, 'Where has it gone?'. When your baby is looking at you, bring it back to the front and say, 'Here it is!'.

TAKING TURNS

STAGE
Before words

LEARNING OPPORTUNITIES
- To reach for an offered object
- To take turns in play.

YOU WILL NEED
A ring stacker or similar toy; plastic bowl.

Ring turns

Sharing the game

- Sit opposite your baby, so that your faces are at the same level.
- Let your baby play with the ring stacker for a few minutes. Encourage her to explore the toy and practise removing the rings from the post and replacing them. Do not worry if she does not put them on in the correct size order.
- Now, replace all the rings on the stacker. Remove the first ring and say, 'Mummy's turn', then place it in the bowl. (Keep the bowl out of your baby's reach.) Next, help your baby to remove a ring and hold out your hand for her to give it to you. Say, '(*Your baby's name*)'s turn'. Take the ring and place it in the bowl.

- Repeat with 'Mummy's turn', and then with '(*Your baby's name*)'s turn'. Pace the game so that your baby has enough time to remove the ring and give it to you, but not so much time that her attention starts to wander. Emphasise the turn-taking words.
- When all the rings are removed, praise your baby and shake the bowl of rings to gain her attention. Offer her one of the rings and help her to replace it on the post. Again, stress the turn-taking words, for example, '(*Your baby's name*)'s turn', then 'Mummy's turn'.

Taking it further

- Play this game in the bath or water tray and enjoy some bubbly turn-taking!
- Roll the rings along the floor to your baby. Say, 'Ready, steady...', then wait for her to make a sound or say, 'Go!', before you send a ring to her.

TAKING TURNS

LEARNING STAGE
Before words

LEARNING OPPORTUNITIES
- To take turns to make sounds
- To babble using the same syllable two or three times, for example, 'da da' or 'ga ga'.

YOU WILL NEED
A hand-held safety mirror; baby yoghurt or similar.

Baby talk

Sharing the game

- Your baby will love looking at his and your reflections in the mirror. Hold the mirror in front of you and your baby so that you can both see each other's faces clearly.
- Show your baby, by smiles and touches, how pleased you are when he joins in with his own sounds. Sing:

  Look in the mirror, who do I see?
  I see (*your baby's name*) looking at me.
  Look in the mirror, who do I see?
  I see (*your baby's name*) looking at me.
  Boo!

- Pause in the middle of the song and continue when your baby makes a sound or reaches for the mirror.
- Listen to the sounds that your baby makes and copy them. Pause and wait for him to have his turn, then continue. After a short while, introduce some variety to the sounds. Focus on the turn-taking as your child develops his baby talk.
- Put a little yoghurt on the end of your nose. Smile at your baby and copy the sounds that he makes as he tries to wipe the yoghurt from your reflection in the mirror. If he is really enjoying this game, let him dip a finger in the yoghurt and put it on your face, then look back in the mirror. Sing the mirror song again, but this time sing:

  Look in the mirror, what do I see?
  I see (*your baby's name*) looking at me.
  Look in the mirror, what do I see?
  I see (*pause and gasp*) my nose!

Taking it further

- Play this game with a baby's play mirror in the bath with bubbles.

TAKING TURNS

STAGE
Before words

LEARNING OPPORTUNITIES
- To imitate actions
- To use actions and own sounds to gain attention.

YOU WILL NEED
Kitchen pots and pans; wooden and plastic spoons; shoebox; large plastic juice bottle; rug.

Beat the drum

Sharing the game

- Place the pots, pans, spoons, shoebox and juice bottle on a rug on the floor.
- Stand back and let your baby explore the objects. Let her try out the different sounds that she can make. Try not to direct her play, except to keep her safe and focused on the activity on the rug.
- Watch carefully to see which of the sounds interest your baby the most and think of any that she has not yet discovered. Look for her favourites – which ones does she keep going back to?
- When your baby is ready, gather the objects together and remove all of them except two of her favourite sound-makers and one that she is yet to discover. Kneel down so that you are on the same level as your baby.

- Use your own spoon as a beater and copy the sounds that your child makes. Wait for her to pause between actions and copy them, for example, if she has been giving one short bang on the pan, do the same. If she has been tapping the pot repeatedly, wait until she pauses, then copy what she has just done.
- Your baby will be fascinated by you copying her. She may make new sounds then look to you to copy them.
- Show your baby new sounds that she can make, for example, by running the wooden or plastic spoons up and down the plastic bottle. Encourage her to copy what you are doing.

Taking it further

- Have just one pan and two beaters and take it in turns to beat the 'drum'. Tap different parts of the pan, loudly and softly, and help your baby to copy your actions.

TAKING TURNS

STAGE
First words

LEARNING OPPORTUNITIES
- To build first-words vocabulary
- To recognise pictures of familiar objects.

YOU WILL NEED
A collection of familiar objects such as a toy car, book, brush, hat, cup and keys; large cardboard box to make a post-box; photographic book of first-words objects.

Pop it in the box

Sharing the game

- Let your child explore the collection of objects.
- Gather the objects together and choose a group of three objects. Sit on the floor with your child and put these objects between you and your child.
- Ask your child to find a particular object and post it in the box. Be sure not to inadvertently give him a clue, such as by looking or pointing at the object. Next, it is your turn, so ask your child which one you should post in the box.
- If your child does not choose an object for you to post, watch him carefully and ask him to choose again. Help him to reach for or point to the object of his choice. Model the word clearly, for example, 'keys', then say, 'Keys in the box' and post them.
- Continue taking turns to play the game. Help your child to listen for, and understand, the names for the objects, then when it is your turn, help him to make choices and use first words.
- When your child has found the object that you have asked for, help him to match it to the photograph of the same object in the picture book, before posting the object in the box.

Taking it further

- Play the game again, this time asking your child to find the object from you describing its use. For example, place the brush, hat and spoon in front of your child and say, 'Show me what you use to eat your dinner'. Emphasise the key words 'eat' and 'dinner' so that your child can find the spoon. Speak clearly, remembering to use your child's name first to gain his attention.

TAKING TURNS

STAGE
First words

LEARNING OPPORTUNITIES
- To take part in a turn-taking game
- To say own name.

YOU WILL NEED
A large cardboard tube; a number of different-coloured balls that will easily fit down the tube; two small cushions; plastic bowl or box.

Here we go!

Sharing the game

- Let your child play putting the balls into the bowl and tipping them out. Ask her to put all the balls back into the bowl by placing each ball into your outstretched hand as you say, 'Ball, please'.
- Give your child the tube and one ball. Show her how to roll the ball down the tube so that it lands between the cushions. Say, 'Ready, steady...', and encourage your child to say, 'Go!' before you or she rolls the ball down the tube.
- Take it in turns to choose a ball from the bowl and roll it down the tube. Ask your child whose turn it is next. Help her by prompting 'Daddy's turn' or '(*Your child's name*)'s turn'.
- Stress the turn-taking part of this game, encouraging your child to say either her name or your name in response to the question 'Whose turn is it?'. If your child is not ready to respond to this question, then help her to respond with a pointing gesture. Show her by pointing, then gently take her hand and help her to form a point, then point to herself and say, '(*Your child's name*)'s turn'.

Taking it further

- Sit opposite your child with her legs and your legs stretched out in front of you. Choose a large, soft ball and gently roll it to your child. Encourage her to roll it back to you. Say to your child, 'It's coming to...' then pause for her to add her name.

TAKING TURNS

STAGE
First words

LEARNING OPPORTUNITIES
- To understand and use action words
- To imitate actions and gestures.

YOU WILL NEED
Two teddies; two cups; two small blankets; two spoons; two brushes; two flannels; two toothbrushes; two shoeboxes.

Shh, Teddy's sleeping

Sharing the game

- Divide the items into matching sets. Put all the items, except the teddies, in the shoeboxes.
- Sit on the floor opposite your child with your faces at the same level. Invite your child to explore the box.
- Take one of the teddies and make it jump into the air. Say, 'Look, Teddy's jumping!'. Give your child the other teddy and say, 'Make your teddy jump – look Teddy's jumping!'. Help your child to imitate the action.
- Next, make your teddy sleep. Cover it with the blanket and say to your child, 'Make Teddy sleep'. Try not to add any further words or interrupt as your child needs time to listen and think. If you interrupt by prompting him too soon, your child may forget what he was planning to do.
- If after a short while your child does need some help, pass him his teddy's blanket and lay your teddy down again. Say to your child, 'Look, Teddy's sleeping'.

- When your child is confidently imitating the actions, put the cup to Teddy's mouth and ask your child to tell you what Teddy is doing. If he responds with an object word, such as 'cup', smile and say, 'Look, Teddy is drinking'. Emphasise the action word.
- Repeat the game with different action words using the other objects from the box.
- Play the game using actions that do not need any familiar objects, such as 'Teddy running'.

Taking it further

- Introduce another soft toy so that your child has to listen and watch for which toy to choose when imitating your actions and listening to the requests in the game.

TAKING TURNS

STAGE
First words

LEARNING OPPORTUNITIES
- To recognise and use animal sounds
- To ask for the animals by sound or name.

YOU WILL NEED
Toy farm animals; cloth bag or empty cushion cover.

On the farm

Sharing the game

- Give your child the farm animals to play with for a few moments. Sing 'Old Macdonald Had a Farm' (Traditional) as she plays.

Old Macdonald had a farm,
E-I-E-I-O!
And on that farm he had some cows
E-I-E-I-O!
With a moo-moo here, and a moo-moo there,
Here a moo, there a moo,
Everywhere a moo-moo!
Old Macdonald had a farm,
E-I-E-I-O!

- Put all the animals in a pile and encourage your child to give you each animal in turn. Ask for it first by the sound that it makes, for example, 'Can you find the animal that says "moo"?'. Hold the bag open for your child to put each animal inside. As she puts the correct animal into the bag, say, 'Yes, the cow says "moo"', then say, 'Bye-bye cow', as it goes into the bag.
- Take the animals out of the bag one by one and before your child can see which animal you have chosen say, 'Look, I have an animal who says…' then pause to attract her attention. Continue with the animal sound, for example, 'baa', then ask your child, 'Who says "baa"?'.
- Take turns with your child to choose an animal from the bag, helping her to name and use the animal sound. Remember to stress the turn-taking part of the game by consistently using the phrase '(*Your child's name*)'s turn'.

Taking it further

- Hide one of the farm animals somewhere in the room and help your child to hunt for it. Make the animal noise as you hunt together. When you find the animal, say to your child, 'Look, it's the (*animal's name*)!'.

TAKING TURNS

STAGE

Putting words together

LEARNING OPPORTUNITIES

- To understand and use some group terms such as food, toys and people
- To follow the rules of a game.

YOU WILL NEED

Two drinking straws; pen; tissue-paper squares; tray.

Your turn next

Sharing the game

- On each of the tissue-paper squares, draw a different item of familiar food (apple, biscuit, sandwich and cake), toys (book, toy car, ball and teddy) and four people (baby, child, parent and grandparent).
- Put some blank tissue-paper squares on to a tray. Show your child how to blow through the straw on to a tissue-paper square so that it blows off the tray. Let him practise this for a short while.
- Put six tissue-paper squares on the tray, including two from each group. Ask your child to choose some food pictures and help him to blow them off the tray. Continue the game adding squares as needed.
- Encourage your child to blow slowly through the straw and to take his time finding the correct squares before beginning the fun of blowing them off the tray.
- Take it in turns and encourage your child to choose a group of objects for your turn.

Taking it further

- Play the game with pictures from other groups, such as animals, clothes and buildings.
- Look at busy pictures in books, for example, street scenes, and encourage your child to find the details. Use group words and help him to look further to discover similarities and differences. Can he see the police officer, the bus driver, the lady walking the dog or the man with the hat?

TAKING TURNS

STAGE
Putting words together

LEARNING OPPORTUNITIES
- To use new object words
- To introduce describing words.

YOU WILL NEED
Shiny paper; foil; wrapping paper; newspaper; treasure objects that are new and interesting to your child such as keys, coin, fir-cone, pen, jewellery, badge, button and toy vehicle; toy animal; larger objects such as toy telephone, clothes and safe items from around the house; cloth bag or empty cushion cover.

Unwrap some treasure

Sharing the game

- Wrap the larger objects in up to four layers of paper. Wrap the smaller items individually, then place them in the cloth bag.
- Play 'Pass the parcel' with the larger parcels, passing the parcel between you and your child as you sing:

  Parcels and boxes, all shapes and sizes
  Heavy and light, backwards and forwards
  What can be inside?
- Encourage your child to guess what might be inside the parcel. Invite her to unwrap the parcel. Use lots of describing words as she unwraps the parcel. Ask questions and make comments that will help her to describe the look and feel of the parcel and its contents.
- Invite your child to take some treasure from the cloth bag. Share her interest as she opens each parcel. Introduce words that describe the texture, feel, colour, weight or size of the object, for example, 'shiny penny', 'blue car', 'large key', 'tiny button' or 'heavy book' and so on.
- Let your child choose some treasure to wrap for you. Unwrap it carefully and help your child to describe the object by offering options to her, such as, 'I wonder if it is going to be rough or smooth' or 'Do you think it feels heavy or light?'.

Taking it further

- Collect and wrap natural treasures from your garden or from places that you visit.
- Save old tickets, badges, postcards and other paper treasure. Place each item in an envelope and play the game with your child, passing the paper treasure back and forth.

TAKING TURNS

STAGE
Putting words together

LEARNING OPPORTUNITIES
- To understand 'in', 'on' and 'under'
- To use phrases including possession, such as 'Jack's cup'.

YOU WILL NEED
A toy tea set; doll; teddy; simple food items such as biscuits or grapes; small table or tray; small jug of water.

Tea-party turns

Sharing the game

- Help your child to set the table or tray for a tea party, with a teacup and plate for Dolly, Teddy, you and himself.
- Give your child a teaspoon and ask him to put it on Dolly's plate. Encourage him to listen to the two key words in your request – 'doll' and 'plate'.

- Next, offer your child another spoon and ask, 'Whose spoon is this?'. Prompt him to use a phrase including possession, such as 'Teddy's spoon'. Continue taking turns to share out the utensils and some of the food.
- Help your child to pour some drinks. Say, 'Let's pour some into Dolly's cup'. Again, prompt your child to use phrases including possession.
- Next, take some of the food items, such as the grapes. Put a grape under one of the cups and ask your child to tell you where it is. Help him to use the words 'in', 'on' and 'under' appropriately.
- Continue the game, taking turns to put the biscuits on spoons, under plates and in cups. Ask your child to tell you where they are. If your child puts the grape in Teddy's cup, then model the correct phrase, 'Look, the grape is in Teddy's cup!'.
- Stress the turn-taking part of the game, keeping your own words as consistent as possible.

Taking it further

- Help your child to make sandwiches and continue playing.

TAKING TURNS

STAGE
Putting words together

LEARNING OPPORTUNITIES
- To follow the rules of a game
- To listen to key words and understand 'in', 'on' and 'under'.

YOU WILL NEED
A toy egg.

Hide the egg

Sharing the game

- Show your child the egg. Encourage her to cover her eyes while you hide the egg around the room. Count together, 'One, two, three, ready or not, here I come!', then begin the egg hunt with your child.
- Provide a commentary as your child hunts around the room, for example, 'No, it's not under the cushion, is it in the box?'. Hunt together for a few moments, emphasising key words related to position, such as 'in', 'on', 'under', 'behind', 'in front of', 'top' and 'bottom'.
- Start to give your child some clues, for example, 'Getting warmer' as she gets closer to the hiding place, or 'Getting colder' as she moves away. Be sure to give your child enough clues so that she finds the egg before she loses interest.
- Take it in turns to hide the egg. When you have found the hidden egg, help your child to describe where she hid it. Provide alternatives such as, 'Was the egg *in* the cupboard, or *under* the cupboard?'.

Taking it further

- Play this game in the garden or the park. Hide a variety of objects – keys and hats are always popular.
- Vary the game by playing with photographs or pictures.
- Look out of the window together and spend some time looking for objects that are in, on or under things, for example, 'The lady is on the bike', 'The car is under the bridge' and 'The sand is in the box'.

CHAPTER 3

LET'S PRETEND

Pretend play is an important part of your baby or young child's early years. It is essential for him to understand and develop language and to be creative, and it is an important step for him on the path to becoming a confident speaker and writer. Pretend play will enable your baby or child to think about past and future events, help him to express how he feels, make stories in his head and invent new ways to look at ideas that interest or concern him. A rich imaginary world is an important escape and release in times of stress and will enhance your child's childhood. The games in this chapter will help you to encourage different types of pretend play.

BEFORE PRETEND PLAY

Your baby's first intentional play will be with you as she enjoys responding to your voice, face and touch. Her first play with objects will be exploratory as she handles, pats, brings to her mouth or throws objects to find out about them. She will gradually start to recognise familiar objects and toys. In time, she will understand their use and also copy how you use them. This recognition of familiar objects, understanding of the use of objects, then imitation of actions are all important steps towards first pretend play.

How you can help

- Enjoy action and finger rhymes with your baby.
- Provide a teddy or doll for your baby to hug.
- Give your baby time to explore familiar objects.
- Make a treasure basket of safe, familiar objects for your baby to feel and explore.

HOME PLAY

Older babies and young children enjoy imitating actions and sharing familiar household tasks. Your child will enjoy copying you as you sweep the floor or wipe the table. He will watch carefully and, in time, imitate simple sequences of actions. He will enjoy using real props, such as a dustpan and brush, but will also gradually enjoy playing with dolls and toy tea sets. Baby play is often very popular and your child will enjoy playing out social sequences such as feeding a baby, then putting the baby to bed.

As well as family and home pretend play, your child will gradually pretend to be people who play a

significant part in his world, such as the postperson bringing letters or a bus driver selling tickets. This can also include familiar situations for your child, such as playing 'Shop', 'Doctors and nurses' or 'Teachers' as he plays out what he recognises as important for others.

Your child will want to pretend-play on his own sometimes, but other times he will need you to join in.

How you can help

- Allow your child to help with tasks around the home.
- Encourage home play with dolls, tea sets and blankets.
- Provide a few real props such as hats, bags and letters, or packets and boxes for your child to play 'Shop'.

SMALL-WORLD CARS AND PEOPLE

Traditional play with toy cars, animals, dolls' houses and small-world people are an essential part of pretend play. Your child will learn that the small toy animal is a symbol of the real animal. This play with small-world objects helps your child to develop sequences of events in her play and allows her to build her own stories and try out new ideas.

How you can help

- Allow plenty of quiet uninterrupted time for your child to enjoy this type of play.
- Make sure that your child gets time to play with these small toys on her own, as well as alongside a sibling or a friend's child.
- Look at books and read stories together that will provide her with lots of stories and ideas for play.

IMAGINATIVE PLAY

Pretend play with small-world objects will later develop to become imaginative play, where your child will use abstract objects to represent props for his play. For example, he may use a kitchen-roll tube as a telescope, or a rug as a boat. Your child will enjoy dressing up and may create complex imaginary worlds with

characters that you recognise from television programmes or stories, or perhaps with entirely imaginary figures. Your child may also create an imaginary friend. This sort of play encourages creativity and discovery and helps your child to think about the world and see new possibilities. Again, your child will need time to play imaginatively on his own but also will want to share his imaginary world with other children.

How can you help

- Provide some simple dressing-up clothes, blankets and boxes.
- Make models and dens together.
- Respect your child's imaginary friends and the privacy of his imaginary worlds.
- Share books, poems and rhymes to give your child plenty of material for stories and play.

Pretend play will help your child to develop a wealth of language and the skills to become creative and reflective. Show your child that you value his imaginative play by giving him the time to play uninterrupted, appreciating his creations and giving praise.

STAGE
Before words

LEARNING OPPORTUNITIES
- To imitate actions and gestures
- To reach for offered object.

YOU WILL NEED
Two teddies; shoebox; tiny cushion; piece of fabric.

Ted in bed

Sharing the game

- Sit on the floor with your baby, ensuring that your faces are on the same level.
- Pick up your teddy and give it a hug. Say, 'Ah, hug Teddy, look, Teddy's tired, ah, hug Teddy'.
- Give the other teddy to your baby. Hold it out and encourage him to reach for the teddy with two hands. Make sure that he is sitting safely and will not topple over if he reaches forwards. Say, '*(Your baby's name)*, look, here's Teddy!'.
- As your baby takes the teddy, hug your teddy again and help him to copy your actions. Say, 'Look, Teddy needs a hug'.
- Encourage your baby to stroke and pat his teddy gently. Sing 'Rock-a-bye Baby' (Traditional) or a similar sleeptime song.

- Tell your baby that your teddy wants to go to sleep and put it in the shoebox with the cover. Make sure that your baby is watching. Call his name to gain his attention and keep him involved by letting him help you to put the teddy to bed.
- Once the teddy is in bed, say to your child, 'Look, Teddy is sleeping, sshh'.
- Wake up the teddy with a hug and put it to one side.
- Help your baby to put his teddy in the bed, and sing the sleeptime song again.

Taking it further

- Encourage your baby to rock the teddy bear gently as you sing 'Rock-a-bye Teddy'.

LET'S PRETEND

STAGE
Before words

LEARNING OPPORTUNITIES
- To understand the use of familiar objects
- To give objects on request.

YOU WILL NEED
Two dolls; spoon or fork, cup, bowl and plate from a toy tea set.

Feeding Dolly

Sharing the game

- Sit opposite your baby so that your faces are on the same level.
- Invite your baby to explore one of the dolls. After a few minutes, sit the dolls next to each other, between you and your baby.
- Give one of the dolls a pretend drink from the cup. Say to your baby, '(*Your baby's name*), look, Dolly is drinking'. Offer your baby the cup and encourage her to give the other doll a drink. Again, say, 'Look, Dolly's drinking'.
- Tell your baby that your doll would like some more. Hold out an outstretched hand and say, 'Cup, please'. Give her plenty of time to respond and help her to release the cup into your hand. If she holds out the cup, but does not let go, gently stroke the back of her hand, repeating the request.

- Repeat the game giving the dolls some imaginary food with the bowl and spoon.
- Take it in turns to feed the dolls. Use simple words and phrases such as, 'Look, Dolly's eating' and each time encourage your baby to return the spoon into your outstretched hand.
- As you play with your baby, sing the following song to the tune of 'Here We Go Round the Mulberry Bush' (Traditional):

  This is the way Dolly has a drink,
  has a drink, has a drink.
  This is the way Dolly has a drink,
  drink, drink, drink.

- Continue playing together and help your baby to play by singing and encouraging her to copy your actions. Your interest will help your baby to stay focused on the activity, and encourage her to begin to recognise these familiar objects and understand their use.

Taking it further

- Cut some seedless grapes in half. Encourage your baby to pick them out of the bowl and pretend to feed them to the dolls.

LET'S PRETEND

STAGE
Before words

LEARNING OPPORTUNITIES
- To wave 'goodbye'
- To repeat own sounds when imitated.

YOU WILL NEED
Plastic toy cars; shoebox.

Brrm, brrm

Sharing the game

- Sit down on on a rug or blanket on the floor with your baby. This will help more mobile and energetic babies to stay in one particular area. It can help them to focus on the play, rather than become distracted by the need to explore further afield!
- Play with the cars alongside your baby. Notice what he does with the cars. If he knows that they are for pushing forwards and backwards, copy his actions and encourage his play with appropriate sounds and phrases, such as, 'Brrm, brrm, here it comes!'.
- If your baby is exploring the car by bringing it to his mouth or tapping it on the floor, gently run your car on the carpet and say, '(*Your baby's name*), look, car, brrm!'.
- As your baby pushes the cars forwards and backwards, call his name to gain his attention, then 'whizz' your car along the floor and off the rug. Say, 'Car gone, bye-bye, car', and wave 'goodbye' to your car. Repeat this and, this time, encourage your baby to join you in the waving 'goodbye' gesture.

- Place the shoebox on its side and crash the cars into it. Listen to the sounds that your baby makes and imitate them. Play alongside him with the cars, copying the sounds that he makes. If your baby repeats the sounds that you have copied, imitate them again.
- Encourage your baby to make different sounds and to take turns with you, making and imitating his own sounds. This turn-taking is an important stage towards developing words.

Taking it further

- Introduce emergency vehicles and siren sounds to your baby.
- Say, 'All gone!' whenever it is appropriate during your baby's day, perhaps when all the bath water has gone or when his bowl or cup is empty at mealtimes.

LET'S PRETEND

STAGE
Before words

LEARNING OPPORTUNITIES
- To imitate simple actions
- To look at familiar objects when named.

YOU WILL NEED
A large, sturdy cardboard box; cushion; shoebox; teddy; hat; cup; book; bunch of keys; sticky tape.

In my car

Sharing the game

- Make a door in the side of the cardboard box and place the cushion inside to make a seat. Tape the open shoebox to the back of the cardboard box to make a boot for the car.
- Invite your baby to climb aboard. Ensure that she is sitting safely in the 'car', then sing the following song to the tune of 'The Wheels on the Bus' (Traditional):

  The wheels on the car go round and round,
  Round and round, round and round;
  The wheels on the car go round and round,
  All day long.
- Help your baby to pretend to steer the car by showing her how to hold her hands out, as you sing the song again.
- Place the hat and the bunch of keys close to your baby. Say to her, 'Let's find the keys'. If she reaches for, or looks at, the keys, say, 'You have found the keys' and give them to her. Make a keyhole in the cardboard box and help her to pretend to start the car.

- If your baby does not reach for, or look at, the keys, call her name and ask her again. Help her to find the keys by passing them to her, saying '(*Your baby's name*), look, keys!', and showing her how to put the keys in the keyhole. Sing the song again.
- Continue the game by letting your baby find the named object from a choice of two. Show her how to use the objects or put them in the boot.

Taking it further

- Invite your baby to find the object that you have named from a choice of three familiar objects.
- Place all the familiar objects in the boot of the car and encourage your baby to pass them to you one at a time as you name each item.

LET'S PRETEND

STAGE
First words

LEARNING OPPORTUNITIES
- To say own name
- To answer yes/no questions.

YOU WILL NEED
A toy telephone.

Hello, hello

Sharing the game

- Give your child the toy telephone and hold your hand to your ear to pretend that you are also on the telephone. Make a ringing sound or say, 'Ring, ring'.
- Encourage your child to answer your call by putting the receiver to his ear. Say, 'Hello, (*your name*) speaking, who are you?'. Wait for your child to respond, before prompting him with 'It's…', then pause before adding your child's name.
- Continue with this play, encouraging your child to say his name.
- Have fun by asking your child lots of silly questions, for example, 'Is it the dog?' and prompting the response 'No'; 'Is it the postman?', 'No', and so on. Eventually say, 'Is it (*your child's name*)?' and prompt him to say 'Yes'.
- Finish by encouraging your child to say 'Bye-bye'.
- Prompt your child's responses carefully, but not too soon. He will need plenty of time to understand the game and to think about what he wants to say.
- Enjoy the humour of the game with your child and use the names of family friends, pets and favourite characters.

Taking it further

- Ask your child, 'Who shall we phone?'. Give him a choice of two familiar people, then use his toy telephone to make the call. Pass the phone to your child to say 'Hello' and 'Bye-bye'.
- Leave the toy telephone out for your child to play with at any time. Toy telephones are a good way of encouraging older babies and younger children's language skills.

LET'S PRETEND

STAGE
First words

LEARNING OPPORTUNITIES
- To make choices
- To name familiar objects.

YOU WILL NEED
Three dolls, teddies or other soft toys; four plastic plates; four plastic cups; tray; basket of familiar food and food-related objects, for example, yoghurt pot, raisin box, biscuit, apple, banana, cup, spoon and bib (choose items that are familiar to your child and that she can handle safely).

Tea-party time

Sharing the game

- Sit the dolls or soft toys on a rug and ask your child to give each of them, including herself, a plate for their dinner.
- Put all of the other items on the tray. Pass your child a cup and ask, 'Can Teddy have the cup?'. Help your child to give the teddy the cup.
- Ask your child what else she thinks that Teddy would like. Help her to look at the objects on the tray and make a choice. As she reaches for the object, gently hold back her hand and say, 'Teddy wants...'. Encourage her to add the object word. If your child hesitates, help her by saying, 'Teddy wants...', then adding the name of the object that she is reaching for.
- Continue playing the game, with your child setting up the tea party. Keep her interested by adding new items, such as a small packet of tiny biscuits, or maybe a small jug of water for her to pour some drinks.
- Offer your child choices of objects and help her to use gestures, pointing and words to tell you what she wants for each toy.

Taking it further

- If your child regularly chooses the same objects, put them out of her reach. When she points to let you know what object she wants, model the word for her, such as, 'Video, please'. Do not push your child to copy words, but spend time talking to and listening to her first words. Speak to her clearly and simply, but naturally.

STAGE
First words

LEARNING OPPORTUNITIES
- To point to body parts on self
- To copy simple actions.

YOU WILL NEED
Washing-up bowl with warm water; doll; baby shampoo; baby soap; flannel; sponge; talc; towel.

THINK FIRST! Never leave your child unattended near to water, even for a moment.

Bathtime for Dolly

Sharing the game

- Give your child the doll to hold. Talk about the clothes and body parts as you help your child to undress the doll, for example, 'Shoes off, let's tickle her toes'.
- Help your child to add the baby shampoo to the water. Pretend to check the temperature of the water, then encourage your child to check it again before putting the doll in the bath.
- Pass your child the flannel. Say, 'Let's wash Dolly's...', pause before choosing a body part such as her face. Help your child to find the correct body part on the doll, then encourage him to show you that body part on him. Say, 'Look, my face, (*your child's name's*) face, Dolly's face', touching the flannel on each one in turn.
- Continue playing the game by helping your child to bath the doll. Encourage him to copy your actions, for example, washing the doll's hair, sponging her legs, drying her and patting on some talc. Finish with your child hugging the doll wrapped up in the towel.
- As you play, look at and name the body parts on the doll, then find the same body part on you and your child.

Taking it further

- Encourage your child to share his bath with the doll. Say, 'Let's wash Dolly's hands' and let your child wash the doll's hands with the flannel, then do the same with your child's hands.
- Let your child help to wash other younger children or babies. Talk about their body parts and encourage him to imitate your actions.

STAGE
First words

LEARNING OPPORTUNITIES
- To use animal names and sounds
- To say and understand 'gone'.

YOU WILL NEED
A shallow box or seed tray; bark chippings or sand; small-world farm animals; plastic pots such as yoghurt pots; plastic floor mat.

Farmyard fun

Sharing the game

- Fill the shallow box or seed tray with the bark chippings or sand. Add the animals and let your child play for a few minutes, burying the animals and uncovering them.
- Sit close to your child on the floor mat and talk about what she is doing. Describe what is happening, rather than ask questions. Wonder aloud where the animals have gone. Emphasise key words and phrases such as 'All gone!', 'Gone!' and 'Here it is!'.

- Fill one of the pots with some sand or chippings and invite your child to push one of the animals into the pot. Say, 'Oh no, it's gone!'. After a moment, give the pot to your child to tip the animal out.
- This time, offer your child a choice of two animals. Encourage her to use the animal's name or the sound that the animal makes to indicate her choice. Continue burying animals in the pots and tipping them out, each time stressing the key word in this game: 'gone'.

Taking it further

- Play this game in the sink with a bowl of bubbles.
- Find a picture book depicting farm animals and match the small-world animals to the pictures.

LET'S PRETEND

STAGE
Putting words together

LEARNING OPPORTUNITIES
- To understand and use words to describe position, such as 'high' and 'low', 'up' and 'down', 'in', 'on' and 'under'
- To answer 'Where?' questions.

YOU WILL NEED
Cushions; blankets; large cardboard boxes; wooden pegs; dolls or teddies; book.

All in the den

Sharing the game

- Explain to your child that you are going to make a house for the dolls or teddies and invite him to help you.
- Look at the blankets and boxes with your child. Use words to describe their size, for example, 'Look, a big box!' or 'This blanket is very long'.
- Observe your child to see which items interest him. Help him to hold the blankets and stretch them over the boxes and cushions to make a den. Let your child push the pegs on to the blankets to hold them in place.
- Give your child choices, for example, 'Should we put the peg up here, or down there?' or 'Should we put the cushion in the box or under the box?'. Your child may respond by looking, pointing gesturing or speaking. Praise him and model the correct phrase, such as, 'Let's put it in the box'.
- When you have made the den, continue playing with your child. Talk about where the items should go, for example, 'Where shall we put Teddy's bed?' or 'Where shall we put the book?'.
- Spend a few minutes sitting in the den with your child, enjoying the enclosed space and perhaps looking at the book together.

Taking it further

- Look at picture books together. Play a 'Can you find it?' game, asking your child to find details in the picture, for example, 'Can you find the dog?'. Your child will often point to the picture. Respond using words to describe the position of the dog in the picture, such as, 'Well done, the dog is in the car'.
- Make the special den a cosy place to play in and share a favourite drink with your child after playing.

LET'S PRETEND

STAGE
Putting words together

LEARNING OPPORTUNITIES
- To make marks on paper and understand that text has meaning
- To take turns.

YOU WILL NEED
Four cushions; three dolls or teddies; small pieces of thin card; pencil; bag; hat.

Tickets, please

Sharing the game

- Place the four cushions in a row, one behind the other, to create a bus, and ask your child to place the teddies or dolls on three cushions. Invite your child to sit on the front cushion.
- Sit close to your child on the floor and encourage her to pretend to be the bus driver, steering the bus. Move her hands and arms around in a circular motion to show the wheels going round. Sing 'The Wheels on the Bus' (Traditional):

  The wheels on the bus go round and round,
  Round and round, round and round;
  The wheels on the bus go round and round,
  All day long.

- Invite your child to help you make some bus tickets. Sit alongside her and use the pencil to write her name, 'Teddy' and 'Dolly' on separate tickets. Give her some other tickets to 'write' on. Allow her to mark the tickets with the pencil in any way she chooses. Do not worry about how she is holding it. Many children, at this stage, will hold a pencil in the palm of their hand. Let her enjoy making the tickets.

- When the tickets are complete, ask your child to put them in the bag. Wear the hat, carry the bag and give each of the toys as well as your child a ticket for the bus ride, while singing 'The Wheels on the Bus' again.
- Encourage your child to take a ticket out of the bag for each of the dolls or teddy bears and one for you. Stress taking turns by saying, 'Dolly's turn', 'Teddy's turn' and so on.

Taking it further

- Talk to your child about where the bus is going. Pretend to take the bus along a bumpy road, helping your child to bounce on her cushion. Let her make Teddy bounce along the bumpy road as well.

LET'S PRETEND

STAGE
Putting words together

LEARNING OPPORTUNITIES

- To imitate actions and add the final word to the end of a familiar rhyme
- To copy simple, everyday jobs from around the house.

YOU WILL NEED
Two large cardboard boxes; marker pen; shoeboxes; small boxes and packets, such as empty cereal boxes and so on; plastic bowls; plastic plates; small pans; wooden spoons; plastic kitchen utensils; pretend food.

Yum, yum

Sharing the game

- Draw four rings and some dials on the base of a large cardboard box to make a pretend cooker. Lay the other cardboard box on its side and open it up to create a kitchen cupboard.
- Place the kitchen utensils in a shoebox and the kitchen packets and cereal boxes in the 'cupboard'. Put the pan on the 'stove'.
- Play alongside your child, pretending to cook the dinner. Describe what you are both doing. Try to avoid asking your child direct questions, but rather comment on what you can see, or perhaps wonder aloud, for example, 'That plate looks hot' or 'I wonder what will be inside the sandwich'.
- Talk about what you are doing, for example, 'Look, Daddy stirring'. Give your child another spoon so that he can copy you.
- Sing or chant the following rhyme to your child and help him to add the names of the food that he has made in the last line.

  Yummy, yummy, yummy,
  That will be scrummy in my tummy,
  Yummy, yummy, yummy,
  What's on the plate?
  It's...

Taking it further

- Encourage your child to 'help' with simple tasks around the home. Give him a duster, or let him help hold the vacuum cleaner handle with you. Invite him to carry a box of dusters and cloths around or let him use a dustpan and brush. All the time, your child will be learning to imitate actions and sharing some special time with you.

LET'S PRETEND

STAGE
Putting words together

LEARNING OPPORTUNITIES

- To use two- and three-word phrases with action words and object words such as 'man sleep', 'drive car' and so on.
- To pull on and off simple clothes.

YOU WILL NEED
Large and baggy items of clothing for dressing up, such as hat, shoes, gloves, jumpers, coat, pyjamas and wellington boots; cardboard box or pillowcase; long mirror.

All dressed up

Sharing the game

- Place all the clothes in the cardboard box or pillowcase. Sit on the floor with your child and invite her to pull one item at a time out of the box. Talk about the clothes using describing words, for example, 'heavy coat', 'big shoes' and so on.
- When your child has taken out three or four items, try some of the clothes on. Put the clothes on yourself and pretend to do a particular action or job, for example, if you have put on the boots, pretend to be digging and say to your child, 'Look, Mummy digging'.
- Allow your child plenty of time to explore the clothes and when she is ready, help her to try some of them on. Encourage your child to be as independent as possible, pulling on simple items and pushing arms through sleeves. When she is dressed up, do an action for her to imitate, for example, a man sleeping or a lady driving.
- If your child does not want to try on the dressing-up clothes, help her to choose something for you to try on.

- Encourage your child to copy your actions. Look in the mirror together and talk about the clothes using describing words and body part names, for example, 'Look at the big shoes on your feet'.

Taking it further

- Give your child a basket to pretend to carry some shopping. Talk about what she is doing and describe the items in her basket.
- Leave the box of dressing-up clothes out for your child to explore. She will gain confidence with dressing up by becoming more familiar with the clothes.

CHAPTER 4

LIVELY TIMES

As well as being important parts of communication, listening and giving attention are key skills that open the door to so much learning.

Even before birth your baby will have been able to hear your voice, and the voices of familiar people around you. Within minutes of birth, babies can turn their heads towards voices. They are already starting to develop the ability to listen and respond to voices and other sounds.

The games in this chapter provide lots of ideas for lively play. They will help to develop early language skills with plenty of opportunities to practise listening and paying attention.

THE FIRST MONTHS

You are your baby's most important plaything. She is able to focus her attention on you and your face, and enjoy social play long before she is interested in objects or toys. She will soothe to the sound of your voice and will look to you for comfort and entertainment as well as for having her physical needs met. This early social play is an important part of looking and listening and there is much you can do to help engage your baby's attention and maintain her interest and listening.

How you can help

- Take time for gentle stroking and tickling games with your baby.
- Sing songs and rhymes to your baby.
- Talk to your baby and combine your words with gentle caresses.
- Hold your baby so that you can gaze into each other's faces.
- Take your baby with you from room to room as you go about your daily routines.
- Give your baby interesting things to look at when you are not with her. Black and white patterned mobiles may be particularly appealing to your baby.

PLAYING WITH OBJECTS AND FIRST TOYS

As your baby learns to reach for, pat and grasp toys and familiar objects such as a cup or flannel, he will quickly discover the joy of exploring play. He will explore the feel and sound that objects can make and, most importantly to him, the effect that he can have on them, and of course, on you! By grabbing the spoon and banging it on his tray, your baby will feel its texture and explore the sounds that it can make as it is banged. He will watch the patterns in the food that he is making and, of course, discover that some sorts of exploratory play can have an interesting effect on the adults around him. Your baby's fascination with familiar objects is an important part in his development of understanding of language. The focus of his attention is not only shared between social play with familiar and responsive people, but also with objects and toys. This early play with first toys is an important step for your baby in understanding his world and also in his learning to focus his attention independently from you.

How you can help

- Make sure that your baby is given some time to explore objects and his toys without interruption.
- Put some familiar objects into a basket for your baby to explore.
- Do not have all of your child's toys out at once. Sometimes, let him rummage around in the toy-box, and other times put just two or three toys on the floor for him to have some unhurried exploration.
- Play alongside your baby, encouraging his play without directing it too much.

LISTENING AND ATTENDING

Gradually, the time that your baby spends with each toy or activity will increase. She will be attending longer to the activities that she chooses, and slowly she will also be able to focus her attention on play and games that you have chosen. With this comes your child's increasing ability to listen and to pick out the most important sounds to tune into, and to ignore background noise and distractions. She will learn to listen and to be attentive when she is spoken to, and she will become aware of sounds within your home and the wider environment.

How you can help

- Join in with your child's play and share her interests – children learn to be attentive when the attention and interest are shared.
- Enjoy music and singing with your child.
- Use a lively but natural voice when talking to your child, saying her name first to attract her attention.
- Stop and listen together to sounds that you can hear at home and when you are out and about.
- Try to reduce distractions and background noise, such as the television or radio.

RHYTHM AND SOUND

Young children continue to be fascinated by stories, music and rhyme. Two- and three-year-olds love songs and games with animal sounds, such as 'Old Macdonald Had a Farm' (Traditional). Your child will increasingly enjoy words that rhyme. He will learn to listen for and identify familiar sounds from the environment and will look for the source of sounds that are out of sight. Your child will be a natural musician and will enjoy making and listening to all sorts of music. The chance to experience and enjoy different rhythms and musical sounds is an important way for your child to listen and to learn about language and sounds.

How you can help

- Share poems, stories and rhymes with your child.
- Listen to and make music often with your child. Let him play with and discover sounds.
- Follow your child's interest. Help him to focus on activities and games by ensuring that much of the time it is of his choosing, but when you choose the activity yourself, ensure that it fits with your child's natural interests and enthusiasms.

LIVELY TIMES

STAGE
Before words

LEARNING OPPORTUNITIES
- To give attention by looking
- To lift arms and reach up to ask to be picked up.

YOU WILL NEED
A comfortable chair; small rug or cushion.

Jiggety jog

Sharing the game

- Sit on a comfortable chair with your baby in your lap facing you.
- Sing this 'Hello' song to your baby, using a tune that you are comfortable with:

  Hello (*your baby's name*), Hello (*your baby's name*),
  Hello (*your baby's name*),
  Hello, hello, hello.

- Bounce your knees up and down to make a gentle jogging motion for your baby. If he enjoys this, sing, whisper or chant this rhyme:

  Jiggety jog, jiggety jog
  Up and down, up and down
  Jiggety jog, jiggety jog
  Here we go again.

- At the end of the rhyme, pause, call your baby's name and ask him if he wants it again. If he looks at you, smile and stroke his cheek and say, 'Again?', then repeat the rhyme.

- Continue playing, pausing at the end of the rhyme and asking your baby if he wants it again. Finish this part of the game when he is still enjoying and attending to the rhyme.
- Next, gently put your baby, facing you, on the cushion or rug on the floor, at your feet. After a moment, smile at your baby, call his name, stretch out your arms towards him and say, 'Up?', using an exaggerated questioning voice so that your baby is clear that he needs to do something or make a sound so that you will pick him up.
- If your baby wants to come up, help him to stretch out his arms in a 'pick me up' gesture, then say, 'Up' and lift him on to your knee for a cuddle.

Taking it further

- Encourage the 'pick me up', raised-arms gesture when taking your baby out of his high chair or pram.

LIVELY TIMES

STAGE
Before words

LEARNING OPPORTUNITIES
- To copy clapping hands
- To focus on and wait for an activity for a few moments.

YOU WILL NEED
Fabric bricks or stacking beakers; small teddy or soft toy.

Knock it down

Sharing the game

- Place all the bricks or beakers in a pile close to your baby. Say her name to gain her attention, then stretch out your hand in a 'give me' gesture and ask your baby to pass you a brick.
- Build a tower, each time asking your baby to place the next brick in your outstretched hand.
- When the tower is built, say, 'Ready, steady, go' and encourage your baby to knock down the bricks. Clap your hands as the bricks fall. Gently help your baby to clap her hands in imitation. Ask, 'Again?', then repeat the game.
- Encourage your baby to wait until the tower is built before knocking it down. Keep her attention on the game by encouraging her to pass the bricks to you. Older babies may point to the brick that they want next. Say, 'Ready, steady, go' each time, and encourage your baby to look at you and say 'Go' before knocking down the tower.
- After several repetitions, keep your baby's attention while playing the game by sitting the teddy or soft toy on the top of the tower.

Taking it further

- Say the clapping rhyme 'Pat-a-cake, Pat-a-cake' (Traditional) with your child. Action rhymes and songs are ideal for helping your baby to focus her attention.
- Sing to your baby to help her listen to your voice and keep her attention as you play.

LIVELY TIMES

STAGE
Before words

LEARNING OPPORTUNITIES
- To make choices
- To respond to simple questions.

YOU WILL NEED
A ball; teddy; book.

THINK FIRST!
This is a game for older babies with good sitting balance who enjoy lively play.

Look at me!

Sharing the game

- Sit your baby in a clear space on the floor and ask him if he would like to come up. Stretch out your arms to him as you speak and encourage him to look at you. Say, 'Up' or raise his arms in a 'pick me up' gesture.
- Swing your baby gently high into the air and then down so that his toes just feel the floor, before swinging him up again. Sing this song to the tune of 'Here We Go Looby Loo' (Traditional) or another rhythm that you are comfortable with:

Ready, and up and down,
Ready, and up and down,
Ready, and up and down,
Up and down, and stop.

- If your baby is enjoying this gentle lively play, repeat the game. If he appears anxious or in any way distressed by the big gentle movements, sit him on your knee, facing you, and hold his hands. Repeat the rhyme moving his hands up and down to the song.

- Next, holding your baby gently but firmly under his arms, move him from side to side and sing this song:

Ready, and side to side
Ready, and side to side
Ready, and side to side
Side to side and stop.

- Repeat the song before giving your baby a choice, then ask him which song he would like. Use actions and gestures to add meaning to your question.

Taking it further

- Spread the ball, book and teddy on the floor, approximately one metre from your baby, and ask him, 'Where is the ball?'.
- Help your baby to find the ball. Hold it and sing the 'Up and down' song, moving the ball up and down as you sing. Ask him to find the other objects. Hold an outstretched hand out so that he can place it in your hand. Sing the 'Up and down' song or the 'Side to side' song.

LIVELY TIMES

STAGE
Before words

LEARNING OPPORTUNITIES
- To keep attention on a game for a few minutes
- To fill and empty a container.

YOU WILL NEED
A plastic bowl or box; selection of familiar objects including spoon, cup, hairbrush, shoe, keys, teddy, book and car.

In and out

Sharing the game

- Let your baby explore the bowl or box. Play 'Peek-a-boo' with it and tap it to find out what sounds it makes.
- Pass one of the objects to your baby and help her to put it on the box. Next, hold up two objects so that she can choose which one she would like. As she takes an object, name it and place it in the box. Continue playing, sometimes putting the objects on the floor for her to pick up before placing them in the box.
- Offer the objects from different sides so that your child needs to reach and grasp accurately with each hand. Remember to offer some larger objects using two hands in the middle.
- Talk to your baby to keep her attention until all the objects are in the box. Offer interesting objects to her and play silly games – for example, you could tip one of the objects off your head and then offer it to your baby.
- If your baby's attention wanders, say, 'Look, (*your baby's name*)' as you offer objects.
- Help your baby to tip all the objects out and start again. Finish the game while she is still interested.

Taking it further

- Help your baby to take the objects out one at a time and pass them to you.
- Play filling and emptying a large cardboard box with big soft toys.

LIVELY TIMES

STAGE
First words

LEARNING OPPORTUNITIES
- To imitate actions and sounds
- To look at pictures and match objects to pictures.

YOU WILL NEED
A picture of an aeroplane, train and car; small toy aeroplane, train and car.

Planes, trains and cars

Sharing the game

- Place the transport pictures on the carpet and give your child the toy car. Say, 'Car' and ask him, 'Where's the car?'. Then say, 'Same?' as you gesture towards the picture. Help your child to find the picture of the car, then hold it next to the toy car and say, 'Car, same'.
- Stand up holding the car and pretend to drive around the room, steering it, beeping the horn and saying, 'Brrm'. Encourage your child to join in with you, either as his own car or holding on to you to be part of your car.
- Next, match the toy train to the train picture, then pretend to be a train on the track, moving your hands to indicate the wheels going round and making train noises. Again, encourage your child to imitate the actions.

- Repeat with the aeroplane. Continue playing this game, encouraging your child to choose which of the pictures he would like, matching it to the object, then together pretending to be that vehicle. Have fun with the sounds and exaggerated actions.
- Keep your child's attention on the game by introducing new sounds and actions, such as by saying, 'Tickets, please' on the train, or being the windscreen wipers moving on the car.

Taking it further

- Play this game with toy animals and matching pictures.
- Share pictures, books and rhymes with your child as often as possible. This will help to give him the confidence to join in.

STAGE
First words

LEARNING OPPORTUNITIES
- To take part in and complete a simple game
- To name familiar objects.

YOU WILL NEED
A cot sheet; selection of familiar objects such as toys, clothes and mealtime or bathtime objects.

Up and down

Sharing the game

- Spread the cot sheet on the floor and help your child to grasp two corners, then hold the opposite corners. Waft the sheet up and down in the air. Hold it as high as your child can reach and say, 'Up, up, up', then 'Down, down, down' as you both slowly bring the sheet down to the floor.
- Choose one of the objects and place it on to the sheet. Lift the sheet together and gently bounce the object up and down in the sheet. Take it as high as you can, then lower it to the floor. Say the 'Up, up, up' and 'Down, down, down' phrases each time.
- Next, invite your child to choose an object to place on to the sheet. Prompt her to tell you what she has chosen. Make the game fun by bouncing the object up and down and sometimes right out of the sheet. Keep the pace at the correct level to hold your child's attention.

- Each time, help your child to choose the object to go on the sheet and encourage her to tell you what she has chosen. Prompt her with the name of the object and also imitate its use – for example, imitate brushing your hair, then say, 'Brush', or hold the spoon to your mouth and pretend to eat, then say, 'Spoon'.

Taking it further

- Ask your child to bring a familiar object from another room to go on to the sheet.
- Put a teddy on to the sheet. Swing the sheet from side to side and sing 'Rock-a-bye Baby' (Traditional).

LIVELY TIMES

STAGE
First words

LEARNING OPPORTUNITIES
- To imitate actions
- To imitate the use of familiar objects.

YOU WILL NEED
A hairbrush; flannel; toothbrush; towel; teddy or doll.

Just like me

Sharing the game

- Stand opposite your child.
- Jump up and down and sing this action song to a tune that you are comfortable with (try to use the same tune each time that you play the game):

  Everybody do this, do this, do this,
  everybody do this, just like me.

- Repeat the song, changing the action each time. Carry out big and lively actions, using humour as well as your child's particular interests to keep his attention. Try actions such as patting your head, clapping your hands, stamping your feet and so on.
- Next, sit down opposite your child and pass him the hairbrush. Pretend to brush your own hair, then help your child to imitate the action using the brush on his hair. Sing the 'Everybody do this' song as you play.
- Continue with the other objects. If your child is reluctant to imitate these smaller actions with the familiar objects, try carrying out the action on a doll or teddy. Help your child to brush the doll's hair, then pretend to brush your own hair and sing the 'Everybody do this' song.

Taking it further

- Invite your child to help you with simple tasks in the home or garden.
- Give your child simple safe tools to play with, such as a dustpan and brush or duster, so that he can imitate actions that he has seen and move towards pretend play.

LIVELY TIMES

STAGE
First words

LEARNING OPPORTUNITIES
- To use first words to ask for objects and name pictures
- To focus attention for a few minutes on an adult-directed game.

YOU WILL NEED
A blanket or rug; hat; coat; pretend food; play torch; string for fishing line; pictures of crocodiles, boats and sea creatures.

All aboard

Sharing the game

- Sit on the blanket or rug opposite your child with your legs stretched out either side of your child to make a pretend boat. Hold hands with your child and sing 'Row, Row, Row Your Boat' (Traditional):

  Row, row, row your boat,
  Gently down the stream;
  Merrily, merrily, merrily, merrily,
  Life is but a dream.

- Tell your child that it is raining and ask her what you need. Show her the hat and coat and prompt her to ask for them. Put on the hat and coat with your child then sing the song again.

- Say to your child that you are hungry and you need to catch a fish. Ask your child to find the fishing line and help pretend to fish from the boat. Set off again, singing 'Row, Row, Row Your Boat'.
- This time, tell your child that it is getting dark and ask her what you need. Invite her to find the torch and shine it on the crocodile picture.
- Sing 'Row, Row, Row Your Boat' again, and this time invite your child to shine the torch on the other pictures, encouraging her to name them.

Taking it further

- Play a similar game pretending to be on a bus and singing 'The Wheels on the Bus' (Traditional).

LIVELY TIMES

STAGE
Putting words together

LEARNING OPPORTUNITIES
- To use and understand 'big' and 'little'
- To wait for the beginning of a game.

YOU WILL NEED
A large toy car or pedal car; small toy car; large cardboard box; shoebox; large beach ball; small ball; chalk.

Big and little race

Sharing the game

- Mark a start and a finish line on the ground outside using the chalk.
- Invite your child to find the big box and place it on the start line. Ask him to put the little box on the start line for you.
- Ask your child to say 'Ready, steady, go', then encourage him to race with you, pushing his box to the finish line.
- Race again with the big and small cars. Make sure that your child understands the words 'big' and 'little' and is using them appropriately. For example, ask him to find the little car, or ask him which car he has, prompting him to use a two-word phrase including the object word and 'big' or 'little' as a describing word.

- Continue playing with your child. Mix and match the objects, for example, race the big ball with the big box, or the big car with the small box.

Taking it further

- Play 'Follow-my-leader' with your child, taking it in turns to imitate each other's actions, for example, giant strides and tiny steps, or big and little jumps.
- Go for a walk and collect pairs of big and little natural objects such as big and little leaves, big and little pebbles and so on.

LIVELY TIMES

STAGE
Putting words together

LEARNING OPPORTUNITIES
● To match and recognise colours
● To take turns and follow the rules of a simple game.

YOU WILL NEED
Four cereal boxes; red, blue, yellow and green paint (or plain coloured paper); paintbrushes; ball; selection of toy cars.

Skittle alley

Sharing the game

● Help your child to paint the front of each box in a different colour. Leave the boxes to dry.

● Next, stand the boxes in a row outside to create a skittle alley. Take turns with your child to roll the ball at the boxes to try to knock them over. Help your child to name the colours as the ball knocks over each box.

● Invite your child to guess which colour box you are going to knock over.

● Next, help your child to find a car of the same colour as each box and stand the cars on the boxes. Play the game again.

● Use simple phrases to stress turn-taking, such as, 'Mummy's turn, now it's (*your child's name*)'s turn'.

● Keep your child's attention focused on the game by going at a steady pace, moving other distracting toys out of the way and letting her know ahead of time when the game will be over, such as by saying 'One more turn and then we've finished'.

Taking it further

● Introduce new colours to the skittle alley.

● Add large and small boxes of the same colour to the skittle alley. Encourage your child to tell you the size and colour of the box that she has knocked down, such as the big red box.

● With your child, use each box to make a collection of objects of that particular colour.

LIVELY TIMES

STAGE
Putting words together

LEARNING OPPORTUNITIES
- To use object and action words together
- To understand and use the describing words 'fast' and 'slow'.

YOU WILL NEED
Eight sheets of A4 paper or thin card; marker pen.

Fast and slow

Sharing the game

- Sit with your child and draw a snail on the first sheet of paper or card. Ask him what it is and whether it will move fast or slow. Together pretend to be slow-moving, crawling snails.
- Draw a tiger on the next sheet of paper or card. Talk about the tiger and how fast it moves. Pretend to be tigers running fast and growling loudly.
- Continue this by drawing a bicycle and a car on two sheets of paper or card, then a hot-air balloon and a plane. Each time talk about 'fast' and 'slow' and pretend to be that object.
- For the last two sheets of paper or card, invite your child to choose something that moves very slowly for you to draw, and then something very fast.
- Now turn all the cards face-down on the floor. Invite your child to choose a card and turn it over. Ask, 'Is it fast or is it slow?'. Shout out together, then pretend to be that object. Take it in turns to turn over the cards. Each time ask, 'Is it fast or is it slow?'.

- Talk about what each object is doing. Encourage your child to use object and action words together, for example, 'plane flying' or 'balloon floating'.
- Before you turn over some of the cards, let your child guess if the object will be fast or slow.

Taking it further

- Look at pictures together, finding things that move fast and things that move slowly.
- Talk about the way that animals and objects move. Use action words and, where possible, pretend to make that action, such as a snake slithering or a frog jumping.

LIVELY TIMES

STAGE

Putting words together

LEARNING OPPORTUNITIES

- To listen to and join in patterns of sound and rhythm
- To take part in a turn-taking game.

YOU WILL NEED

Four sheets of A4 paper or thin card; marker pen; pillowcase.

In the jungle

Sharing the game

- Sit with your child and talk about the animals that you might find in a jungle, or perhaps at a zoo.
- Draw a snake, a monkey, an elephant and a lion on each sheet of paper or card.
- Place all the sheets in the pillowcase and invite your child to pull one out. Mime the action of the animal and make a short pattern of sound for your child to copy.
- For the snake: slither on the floor and make three short hiss sounds, pause, then repeat. Help your child to copy the pattern of sounds. Encourage her to listen carefully and join in with you.

- For the monkey: jump around and make a clapping rhythm of loud and quiet hand claps.
- For the elephant: plod about swinging your arm as a trunk and make slow, stamping noises.
- For the tiger: prowl around, then stop and make two quiet growls followed by a loud roar.
- Each time, help your child to be the same animal, imitating both the actions and the pattern of sounds. Praise her careful listening as well as her imitations.

Taking it further

- Share action rhymes and songs with your child as often as possible.
- Walk around the house together listening to sounds such as the clock ticking, the fridge humming and so on.
- When you are out and about with your child, stop in the middle of town, or perhaps in the park, and spend a few minutes listening carefully together to all the different sounds that you can hear.

LIVELY TIMES

STAGE
Putting words together

LEARNING OPPORTUNITY
- To understand and use words to describe position, size and length.

YOU WILL NEED
Several large cardboard boxes; lengths of fabric; string; ribbon; sticky tape; scissors (adult use); cardboard tubes; toy tool set.

THINK FIRST!
Never leave your child unattended with lengths of string or ribbon.

The building site

Sharing the game

- Play this game in the garden. Open up some of the cardboard boxes to form large flat pieces of card.
- Let your child explore the boxes and other materials. Ask him if he would like to build anything special. Work alongside your child, letting him make the decisions, but help to fix the boxes and card together using string or sticky tape.
- Describe what your child is doing. Emphasise phrases that include positional words such as 'in', 'on' and 'under'. Ask questions such as, 'Shall we put this bit under the box or on it?' or 'Where should we fix the string?'. Try to ask questions that need more than a 'yes' or 'no' as an answer.
- Talk about long and short pieces of ribbon or cardboard. Work with your child using the toy tool set to make holes in the card so that he can thread the string through to fix the pieces together. (Children will often decide what they are going to make when the project is under way and will adapt their plans as they go along.)

Taking it further

- When the construction is complete, sit with your child and talk about how it was made. Remember together the sequence, prompting your child to recall what he did and how you solved any difficulties encountered along the way.
- Provide some props to enable your child to continue playing with his construction. If he has built a house, offer a tea set or perhaps a blanket for a bed. If he has built a rocket, give him an empty carton and pretend that this is rocket fuel, and so on.

LIVELY TIMES

STAGE
Putting words together

LEARNING OPPORTUNITIES
- To answer a simple question
- To use an object word and an action word together, such as 'plane flying'.

YOU WILL NEED
Two sheets each of A4 paper, thin card and kitchen foil; two shoeboxes.

High and low

Sharing the game

- Sit alongside your child and talk about things that fly in the sky, such as aeroplanes, birds, kites, hot-air balloons and so on.
- Make two very simple paper aeroplanes using the two sheets of paper, then repeat with the card and the foil.
- Count the planes into the two shoeboxes together so that you have one of each in each shoebox.
- Have a shoebox each and take it in turns to launch your planes, talking about flying high or flying low. Focus on taking turns. Encourage your child to wait for her turn and to say 'Ready, steady, go' before launching the plane.
- Help your child to think ahead and guess which plane might fly high in the air. Talk about where the planes might land.
- At this stage, children will often use short phrases to talk about familiar objects, real to them and also in the 'here and now'. Thinking and talking about things that have happened previously, or may happen in the future, are much more difficult and this game will provide a fun way to help your child to predict what might happen, then test out her ideas straight away.

Taking it further

- Fly a kite together and marvel at the height that it achieves.
- Go for a walk around your local environment with your child. Can you spot any really high buildings or tall trees?
- Sing 'The Grand Old Duke of York' (Traditional) together, bending down low and then stretching up as high.

CHAPTER 5

Going out and about in your local area will provide endless opportunities for your baby or young child to learn and develop her communication skills. Children who are confident speakers and effective communicators have many of the skills that they need to learn, both independently and as part of a group. Confidence and a range of speaking and listening skills will be the bedrock of learning and will help your child to form rewarding relationships with other children and adults. The games in this chapter provide lots of ideas and tips for making the best use of the area available to you to develop your child's language skills.

OUT AND ABOUT

EARLY CONFIDENCE

Your baby's preverbal language skills depend on him forming positive rewarding and stimulating relationships with you and other people that care for him. His skills develop through social play with those of greatest significance to him. Confidence comes from positive regard and the way in which people respond to him. He needs consistency in the responses that he gets to his early communication, as well as stimulation to ensure that he remains alert. His inborn drive to communicate and desire to understand the world and those around him, should be nurtured. He needs people to enjoy him and to respond to him with warmth and encouragement.

How you can help

- Enjoy social play with your baby, holding, hugging and making eye contact.
- Share tickling games, rhymes and songs with your baby.
- Look at books with your baby – it is never too early to start.
- Enjoy music together. Try to listen to as many different styles as possible.
- Talk to and sing to your child. If others care for him, ensure that they are spending time doing all this, too.

TUNING IN

Tuning into your child's early communication and play will help her to develop a positive approach to language and social play. It will enable her to form positive relationships with adults and other children. It will enable you to have a good understanding of her, help you to know what motivates and encourages her, and what she finds less rewarding and boring. It will build trust between you and allow you to support her as she meets new situations and challenges and overcomes obstacles. Listening closely to how and why your child's language is said means that you are better placed to communicate effectively with her. If you listen to her, she is more likely to listen to you. If you share her interests and respect her opinions, she will be inclined to accept your suggestions and guidance.

How you can help

- Share your child's special interests and show her what interests you.
- Take time to listen to and relax with your child.
- Respect the choices that your child has made.
- Have fun together and talk about your shared enjoyment.
- Listen carefully to what your child is saying and try not to talk about your child when she can hear you.

FAMILIAR PEOPLE AND PLACES

Your child will be most confident in familiar places and with people he knows. This is of great significance, because when he is feeling most secure and has positive consistent relationships with the most important people in his life, he will gain the confidence to explore and develop new skills. He will need new and stimulating experiences, but not too much too soon. He needs to be allowed to develop at his own pace and for his progress to be recognised and praised. Children gain confidence from being successful and having their achievements recognised. As he develops and matures his interests, your child will become less home-based and will become increasingly interested in people who are important in his world, such as the postman or doctor, and in places that are familiar and safe but offer new possibilities and opportunities.

How you can help

- Give your child uninterrupted time to play and explore.
- Talk to your child using a rich and varied vocabulary.
- Share books, rhymes, poems and songs with your child.
- Make the most of familiar routines and everyday situations at home and in your local area to help develop your child's confidence and language skills.

RICH LANGUAGE ENVIRONMENT

Sharing and enjoying picture books, story-books, music, poems, rhymes and action songs is one of the best ways of developing your child's confidence with language. It will help to develop her creativity and support development of her listening and attention skills. It will encourage your child to be an active listener and effective communicator. All this will benefit her early literacy skills. Sharing your child's enthusiasm and providing new information and opportunities to support her developing interests will help to enhance her understanding of the world. Make the most of your local library and the opportunities that it offers for your child to hear stories, look at books and join in with music and song times.

How you can help

- Recall events from the past and talk about the near future with your child. Comment and wonder, ask questions and respond to those that your child may have.
- Be animated, attentive and interesting. Ask your child open questions that need more than a 'yes' or 'no' answer.
- Listen carefully to your child and try to avoid interrupting or hurrying her speech.
- Read to your child and provide as much opportunity to look at and share books, stories and pictures as possible.
- Make up stories and nonsense rhyming words together.
- Value your child's contributions and respect her efforts.

OUT AND ABOUT

STAGE
Before words

LEARNING OPPORTUNITIES
- To listen to and enjoy rhyming words
- To ask for more with a glance, smile or gesture.

YOU WILL NEED
A bath or swimming-pool.

Splish, splash, splosh

Sharing the game

- If you are going to play this game during your baby's bathtime, hold him securely with one arm, and with your other hand hold his hand to share the songs and actions. If you are going to play the game in a swimming-pool, hold your baby, facing you, supporting him securely under his arms in the pool.
- Sing this song to a tune that you are comfortable with:

  Splish, splash, splosh,
  (*Your baby's name*) is in the wash,
  Splish, splash, splosh,
  (*Your baby's name*) is in the wash.
- Gently swing your baby from side to side, smiling and watching him carefully to ensure that his is enjoying the actions and song.
- If he smiles and makes sounds to show that he is enjoying the game, ask him, 'Again?'.

- Pause, then smile and say, 'Again?' and repeat the song.
- Your baby may respond with a look or a tug of your arm, or perhaps with smiles or laughter.

Taking it further

- Add another song or rhyme that your baby enjoys, for example, 'Round and Round the Garden Like a Teddy Bear' (Traditional).
- Encourage your baby to let you know which song he would like. He may respond by shouting excitedly when you name the song of his choice or by pulling your hand for the tickling game, or perhaps rocking from side to side for the 'Splish, splash, splosh' song.

STAGE
Before words

LEARNING OPPORTUNITIES
- To anticipate an action
- To enjoy familiar rhymes and songs.

YOU WILL NEED
An indoor or outdoor swing (at home or in the park).

Swing play

Sharing the game

- Fasten your baby securely in the swing seat. Position yourself so that you are at eye level with your baby.
- Swing your baby gently and sing this song to her to a tune that you are comfortable with (as you sing, follow the swing back and forth so that you remain in close eye contact with your baby, smiling and singing to her, as she swings backwards and forwards):

  Swinging, swinging, (*your baby's name*) is swinging
  Backwards and forwards and this is where we stop!

- At the end of the song, hold the swing still in the air, then using an exaggerated but gentle voice, build anticipation saying, 'Ready, steady... go!' before releasing the swing and repeating the song.
- After a few repetitions, swing your baby backwards and forwards for a few moments without singing, then call her name gently to gain her attention. When she is looking at you, say, 'I'm coming to tickle you' and slowly move towards her and tickle her gently on the arm.
- When you are confident that she is enjoying the game, tickle her on her tummy or perhaps under her chin.

Taking it further

- Older babies may enjoy the gentle rocking motion of a rocking horse or similar toy.
- Again, share your child's enjoyment of this game by singing to her and stopping often so that she has to ask for more with a sound, glance or action, or perhaps by copying or saying 'More' or 'Again'.

OUT AND ABOUT

STAGE
Before words

LEARNING OPPORTUNITIES
- To look at familiar objects as they are named
- To point to objects to ask for them.

YOU WILL NEED
A shopping bag; familiar shopping objects such as keys, book, apple, letter, packet of biscuits, carton of yoghurt and so on.

In the bag

Sharing the game

- Sit on the floor with your baby.
- Give each object to your baby for him to explore. Encourage him to reach and grasp with two hands for larger objects and to move objects from one hand to another.
- Hold open the shopping bag and encourage your baby to release the object into the bag. If he is reluctant to let go, stroke the back of his hand and say, 'Thank you'. As he releases the object from his hand and it falls into the shopping bag, say, 'Gone!'.
- Continue with this for three more objects, then leave two or three objects, such as the biscuits, nappies and yoghurt, within easy view but out of your baby's reach. Ask, 'Where's the yoghurt?' and encourage your baby to look towards, reach for or point towards the named object.
- As you name the object, point to it and pass it to your baby for him to feel before putting it in the bag, saying, 'Gone!'.

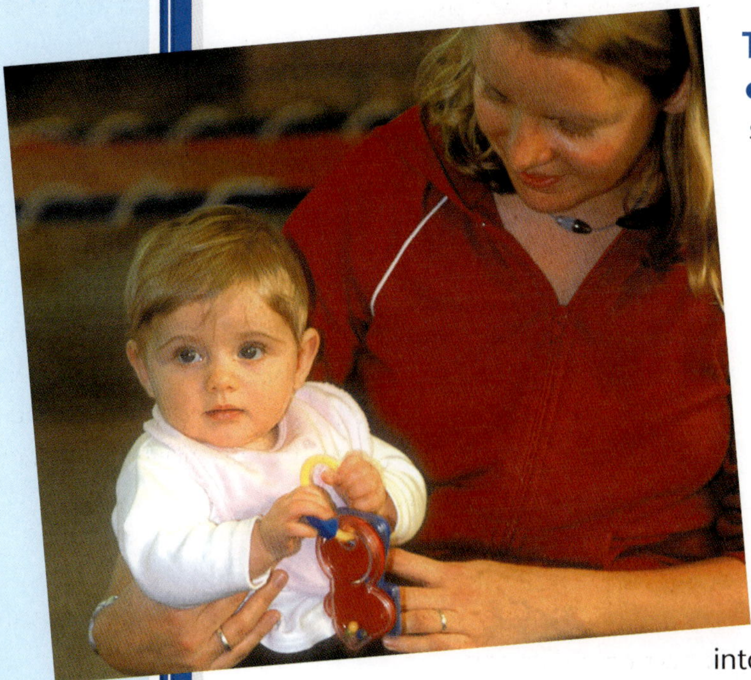

Taking it further

- If possible, play the game at a supermarket.
- Ensure that your baby is securely fastened in the shopping trolley and, as you go around the supermarket, talk to your baby about what you can see.
- Pass your child some of the items for him to feel and explore.
- Encourage your baby to reach for and grasp objects and also to pass them back into your outstretched hand. This will help to build on his understanding of gesture and early communication, and also to widen his experience of exploring a variety of objects.

STAGE
Before words

LEARNING OPPORTUNITIES
- To use a pointing gesture
- To make a choice.

YOU WILL NEED
Garden or park; small plastic bowl or play bucket; wellington boots if appropriate.

Off we go!

Sharing the game

- If your baby is walking, help her to step on the grass and stamp through leaves or puddles. Allow her as much freedom for safe exploration as possible.
- Pick up two natural objects that would be safe for your baby to hold, such as different leaves. Offer both of them to your baby and encourage her to point to the one that she would like. If she reaches, gently form her hand and finger into a point and touch her pointing finger on to the object and say, 'This one, you would like this one'.
- Allow plenty of time for your child to explore the leaf and to feel the texture. Blow on the leaf and throw it into the air for her to watch it fall. Return the leaf to her so that she can copy your actions or make new discoveries.

- Hold the bowl or bucket out for your child to place the leaf in. Help her to release the leaf by gently stroking the back of her hand and saying, 'In it goes!'.
- Continue going around the garden or park collecting natural objects, using a pointing gesture for your baby to make choices. Allow plenty of time for her to explore, then let her practise placing the objects in the bowl or bucket.
- Take the objects home and let your baby explore them, playing at emptying and filling the bucket with the objects that you have collected together.

Taking it further

- Point to show your child objects in the distance, for example, a bird or an aeroplane.
- If your child tries to show you an object in the distance by reaching and vocalising excitedly, share her interest and model a distance pointing gesture.

OUT AND ABOUT

STAGE
First words

LEARNING OPPORTUNITIES
- To imitate actions
- To use actions and first words together.

YOU WILL NEED
Your local area.

Around my town

Sharing the game

- Go for a walk with your child around your local area. Help him to look at what is around him by playing a game of 'I can see'. For example, he could see a car, bicycle, dog, window cleaner and so on.
- As you spot objects or people for your child to name, say, for example, 'I can see a car'. Stop and wait for your child to point to the car. Say, 'Car' again and pretend to be steering a car. Encourage your child to copy you by saying to him, 'Can you drive the car like me?'.
- If your child makes an attempt to say or imitate the word 'car', praise him by saying 'Yes, good boy, car'.
- Continue playing the game, spotting familiar objects or people and playing out actions. Each time encourage your child to join in with the actions.
- If your child is able to find and name the objects with ease, encourage him to use an action word and an object word together in a phrase with two key words. For example, if he has found and said 'dog', then say, 'Yes, well done, the dog is barking'. The key words would be the object word and action word, for example, 'dog barking'.

Taking it further

- Look at some picture books together and find the objects that you have spotted on your walk. Encourage your child to do the actions and label the pictures.
- Go for a walk and take a picture book with you. Match the items that you see with the pictures in the book.

STAGE
First words

LEARNING OPPORTUNITIES
- To match objects and pictures
- To understand and use the word 'same'.

YOU WILL NEED
Packets and wrappers from regular items that you buy at a supermarket; scissors; glue; pieces of A5 card; small bag; trip to the the local shops or supermarket.

Match the object

Sharing the game

- Trim some of the wrappers and glue them to the pieces of card. Show them to your child and talk about the different objects. Match them to the real food items in the kitchen, for example, the wrapper from the bread to the bread in the tin.
- Spread the cards out on the floor. Invite your child to find each item by name, then to place each one in the bag.
- Leave the cards and bag around your home for your child to play with and for you to talk about together. Encourage her to match the cards with items as you are using them.

- Take the bag of cards on a shopping trip and help your child to match the items that you buy to the items that are on the cards.
- Tell your child which item you are going to buy next, so that she can find it in the bag and hold it until you have found the item that you need.
- Each time your child matches an item to the picture, say, 'Look, same'. Match object to object by holding a second identical item next to the first and say, 'Same', then hold one next to the picture on the card and say, 'Same'.

Taking it further

- Make a second matching set of the cards and help your child to find matching pairs.
- Take every opportunity to match objects and pictures. Use the word 'same' consistently. Look for matching pairs around the home, such as socks, shoes, cups, spoons and so on.

OUT AND ABOUT

STAGE
First words

LEARNING OPPORTUNITIES
- To recognise simple line drawings
- To take turns and wait for the start of the game.

YOU WILL NEED
A park or large open space; six sheets of thin A4 card; marker pen.

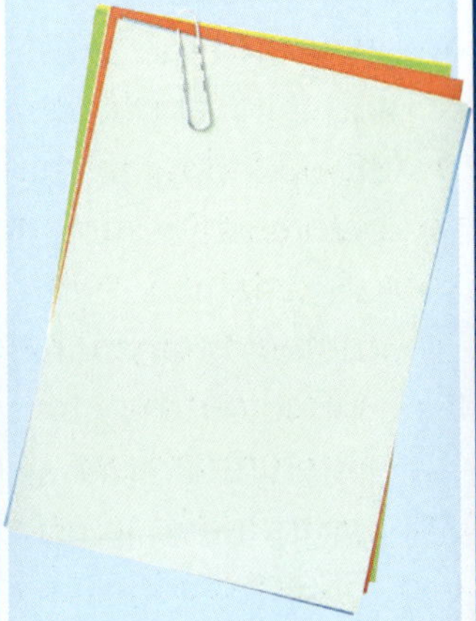

Race you!

Sharing the game

- Look around the park or large open space with your child and ask him to tell you what he can see. As you talk about what you can see, choose six objects that you would be able to race to, for example, a tree, fence, slide, signpost and so on.
- Make a simple line drawing of each item on a piece of card. Shuffle the cards and spread them out face-down on the grass. Invite your child to go first to choose one of the cards. Encourage him to tell you what is on the card. Stand together, say, 'Ready, steady, go!', then race to the matching object that is shown on the line drawing on the card.
- Take it in turns to turn over the cards. Help your child to name the object that he can see in the line drawing and encourage him to point to where the matching object is. Use single label words as well as descriptive two-word phrases, such as 'tree' and 'tall tree'.
- Listen for and use two-word phrases that link an action word with an object word, and two-word phrases that combine a describing word with the object word, such as 'boy crying' and 'red slide'.

Taking it further

- Play a game of matching line drawings to actual objects in other places that you visit, for example, a café or library.
- Look in the library for books with a variety of pictures, photo books, line drawings, bright, simple illustrations or perhaps pictures with lots of detail to look at. Talk about them with your child.

OUT AND ABOUT

STAGE
First words

LEARNING OPPORTUNITIES
- To listen for and recognise familiar sounds
- To use object and action words together.

YOU WILL NEED
A shoebox; pictures or drawings of people and objects that make a noise that you are likely to see in your local area, such as a car, clock, shoe, bird, dog, people talking, baby crying, children playing and so on.

Listen!

Sharing the game

- Look at the pictures or drawings with your child. Talk together about them and see how many your child is familiar with. If she names the picture with an object word, then add an appropriate action word. For example, if she says, 'Baby', respond with, 'Yes, aah, baby crying'.
- Put the pictures in the shoebox and take them with you and your child on a listening walk around your area. Walk slowly and listen together to the sounds that you can hear. Encourage your child to stop and listen to the sounds.

- Give your child plenty of time to listen and think about what the sound might be before suggesting to her what it is. Notice the loud transport sounds and try to listen for animal sounds and people sounds.
- Match the sounds that you hear to the picture cards in the shoebox. Talk about the sounds together. Sit in the park or garden and listen quietly for a few moments. Can you hear birds singing, people chatting, footsteps and traffic sounds?

Taking it further

- Take your child to visit a really quiet place, such as a corner of a garden or park, and listen to the sounds. Copy the sounds that you can hear with your child.

STAGE
Putting words together

LEARNING OPPORTUNITIES
- To match and name colours
- To follow the rules of a simple game.

YOU WILL NEED
A shoebox; scissors; sheet of A4 card; coloured felt-tipped pens; trip to the shops.

It's the same!

Sharing the game

- Cut a slot in the lid of the shoebox to make a simple posting-box.
- Cut the sheet of A4 card into eight squares. Colour pairs of card squares so that the squares in each pair are the same colour, for example, red, blue, yellow and green.
- As you get ready to go out, help your child to look at the clothes that you are both wearing and match the colours on the cards to anything that you are wearing that is the same colour. Use two-word phrases, such as 'red shoes' and 'blue hat'.
- Let your child hold the posting-box as you walk to the shops. Give him one of the colour cards to hold and, as you walk, help him to find an item of the same colour, for example, a red post-box. As he finds an object that matches the colour on the card, encourage him to post the card into the posting-box.
- Choose another colour card and continue playing the game, matching a variety of objects that he sees to the colour cards. Encourage your child to name the colours and to use two-word phrases. If he is using two words together confidently, model three words together by adding an action word, such as 'blue bus stopping', or by adding another describing word, such as 'big yellow crane'.

Taking it further

- Make some more cards and choose different colours to find and match.
- Take the cards with you on a car journey or on a bus and encourage your child to spot people wearing clothes of a particular colour, or cars of that colour, or perhaps a variety of front doors that match the colours on his cards.

OUT AND ABOUT

STAGE
Putting words together

LEARNING OPPORTUNITIES
- To use number words to three
- To recognise red, blue, yellow and green.

YOU WILL NEED
Four small squares of felt or plain fabric, one each of red, blue, yellow and green; car or bus journey.

Count one, two, three!

Sharing the game

- Before you go out in the car or on the bus, give your child the colour squares to look at. Then ask her to cover her eyes with her hands while you hide the squares around the room.
- Help your child to find the squares and name the colours. Talk about things that you might see on your journey that will be of that colour, for example, a red bus or the yellow coat of the crossing-patrol attendant.
- Take the colour squares with you on your journey. Invite your child to choose a square, then choose an object to look for, such as a car, door, coat, shop and so on. Choose objects that you will see plenty of and that you will be able to quickly count three of the chosen colour. Tell your child what you are looking for, such as red cars, and let her hold the red square.
- Together find and count three red cars. Use simple repetitive phrases, for example, 'One red car, two red cars, three red cars'.
- Continue to play the game, choosing other colours and other objects to count. Let your child hold the colour square each time. This will help her to remember what you are both looking for.

Taking it further

- Look for and talk about patterns of colours that you see with your child, for example, striped patterns, and help her to talk about the colours of the stripes.
- Play a 'Find the colour and number' game with your child on your journey – for example, ask your child to find two red lights or three black taxis.

OUT AND ABOUT

STAGE
Putting words together

LEARNING OPPORTUNITIES
- To use group words such as 'toy', 'animal', 'clothes' and 'food'.
- To explore and match textures.

YOU WILL NEED
Old magazines, brochures and catalogues; child-safe scissors; glue; four pieces of card; trip to the shops.

Texture trail

Sharing the game

- Sit with your child and look at the pictures in the catalogues, brochures and magazines. Tell your child that you would like to find some pictures of food.
- Turn the pages together and help him to find the food items. Encourage him to look at a variety of food items, including fruit, vegetables, packets of food, cheese and eggs, so that he understands that all these items are food. Choose a few pictures of food to cut out and paste on to one of the pieces of card.
- Do the same for clothes, toys and animals. As you talk about the pictures, make it enjoyable for your child. Ask him about his favourite toy and tell him what your favourite toys were as a child. Talk about the clothes that he is wearing today. Discuss any animals that you have seen, any pets that your child may have and so on.
- Take the cards with you on a trip to the shops. Ask your child to choose a card, then spend a few minutes looking at, for example, animals in a pet shop, or toys, clothes and food in the appropriate shops.
- Let your child hold the matching card as you explore that shop. Spend time feeling different items and using words to describe the feel and texture of them. Invite your child to feel a wide variety of textures and encourage him to think about other things that may feel the same.

Taking it further

- Go on a barefoot walk around your home with your child to find and talk about the different textures that you can feel, for example, the soft rug, the hard wall, the cold of metal, the cool, smooth plastic bricks and so on.

OUT AND ABOUT

STAGE
Putting words together

LEARNING OPPORTUNITIES
- To find familiar stories and books
- To find details in complex pictures.

YOU WILL NEED
Your local library.

At the library

Sharing the game

- Before you go out, ask your child to bring you her favourite books. Spend a few minutes asking her about the books and showing her which are your favourite ones. Point to the pictures and pages that you like and talk about why you like them.
- Think about your child's special interests and explain that you are going to visit the library to look for books about these topics.
- At the library, let your child explore the books and toys. Encourage her to move around the library, showing her the books full of print in the adult section, the papers and magazines, and then the children's section. Find the pre-school area and show her the picture books.
- Find books that your child is familiar with, then sit and look at them together.

- Show your child books related to her special interests and look out for books with a range of different types of illustrations. Look for photo books and picture books. Many children are fascinated by pictures of babies, so this maybe a good place to start.
- When you have found some books that interest your child, sit with her and encourage her to turn the pages one at a time. Talk about the pictures and look for details for her to find within the picture. Ask her to find objects in the picture and also to tell you what the people or animals are doing. Encourage your child to use action words and describing words as well as words that name or label an object.

Taking it further

- Use your child's books at home to create a pretend library with slips of paper and old envelopes as the library tickets, and a bag to carry the books home.

CHAPTER 6

Babies and young children are sociable beings who enjoy the company of trusted and familiar adults, as well as playing alongside, and interacting with, other babies and young children. Your baby will become increasingly sociable and demanding in her relationships. She will test out these relationships to discover the effects that she can have on the important people in her world. Your child will be keen to form new relationships with other young children as well as trusted adults. Playing the games in this chapter with your baby and child's friends will help to develop positive and purposeful social play.

FRIENDS TOGETHER

YOUR SOCIABLE BABY

Babies are naturally sociable and your baby will actively seek to engage your attention and develop a special relationship with you and other trusted and familiar carers. Within the first few months, he will smile, watch your face, copy facial expressions and take turns with you in baby talk. He will be actively seeking to share your world, and there is much that you can do in the early months of his life to help him.

How you can help

- Make sure that you provide good head support by tilting your baby's chair or cradling his head so that he can enjoy face-to-face play without working hard to hold his head up.
- Around the first three months, your baby will focus on faces approximately 20cm away. Bring your face close to your baby for him to see and explore during your play and cuddles.
- Copy your baby's facial expressions and actions in the early weeks. Be animated and lively, but sensitive to his mood.
- Develop your own special routines and games at home. For example, you could walk your fingers up your baby's chin, then tickle the end of his nose. Make the games predictable and familiar.

DEVELOPING RELATIONSHIPS

Older babies and young children develop an increasing awareness of the influence that they have with other people. They are becoming aware of the plethora of confusing social rules that we live by, and are trying to discover where they fit in this social picture, not just at home but in their wider world of family and friends. At first, your child is trying to fathom why you react in a certain way to a certain action or event, and why the reaction to one particular action varies from person to person. Or indeed, why your reaction may differ on different days or in a different place.

How you can help

- Try to be consistent and clear with your child.
- Tell your child clearly what you would like her to do, rather than focusing on what she should not be doing. For example, say, 'Put the cup on the tray', rather than 'Don't do that' or 'Don't throw your cup on the floor'.
- Be sympathetic and supportive of your child – this is a very confusing time for her. Try to work out why she is acting in a certain way and see it from her point of view.

PLAYING WITH FRIENDS

Your baby and young child has a lot to learn and gain from playing with other children. However, this is also a testing time for him, requiring many new skills such as turn-taking, sharing and negotiating, as well as knowing how to join in with another child's play. Your child will initially play on his own with little obvious spontaneous play with other young children. He may play alongside other children, with each of them absorbed in their own activity. Gradually he will become more watchful as he quietly absorbs the rules of social play. This is an important stepping-stone towards playing co-operatively with another child or as part of a small group.

How you can help

- Make sure that your child has plenty of opportunities to be around other young children and babies.
- Interact positively with other children when you are out and about – your child will take his cue from you.
- Play lots of turn-taking games and encourage your child to share from a very early age.
- Take an active part in your child's play when he is with other children.
- Make time for older children to play with your young child – they can make the allowances necessary for the play to be positive and model positive play behaviour.

THE RIGHT WORDS

Young children need to have the correct words to describe how they are feeling and to understand strong emotions in others. This emotional literacy needs to start early. Your child has to recognise the emotions that she is feeling and know the words to express these. She needs to recognise and be able to name positive emotions such as 'I feel happy', as well as feelings of sadness or frustration. Help your child to recognise when she is feeling tired, or too hot, or cold.

How you can help

- If your child is excited or distressed, use simple words and speak particularly clearly – it will be harder than usual for her to listen.
- On occasions, tell your child how you are feeling and why.
- Talk about feelings and emotions and use simple, clear words to describe them.

FRIENDS TOGETHER

STAGE
Before words

LEARNING OPPORTUNITIES
- To respond to attention by vocalising
- To reach or pat another baby.

YOU WILL NEED
A friend and her baby; two baby blankets.

Roly, poly

Sharing the game

- Invite a friend and her baby to play this game with you. Play the game when the babies can roll confidently from their backs on to their tummies.
- Place each baby on a blanket on the floor. Encourage your baby to lie on his back. Kneel down with him, tickle him and talk to him. Call his name and blow gently on his cheek.
- Sing this song to a tune that you are comfortable with:
  Roly, poly, poly, one, two, three,
  Roly, poly, poly, one, two, three.
- As you sing, help your baby to roll gently on to his side and then on to his tummy, moving towards your friend's baby.
- When your baby arrives next to your friend's baby, appear surprised and say, 'Look, here's (*baby's name*), hello (*baby's name*)'. Take your baby's hand and help him to reach gently for your friend's baby and say again, 'Hello (*baby's name*)'.

- If your baby is enjoying the game, play again. This time gently help your friend's baby to roll over to say 'hello' to your baby. Encourage the babies to reach for each other and gently pat each other to say 'hello'.
- As your baby begins to understand the game, place the babies a little further apart. Help your baby to roll from his back to his front, then right over again to roll a little distance across the blankets to your friend's baby. Each time he rolls over, sing the 'Roly, poly' rhyme.

Taking it further

- Lean a baby safety mirror against the side of an armchair. Help your baby to roll towards the mirror and sing 'hello' to him. Look at his reflection in the mirror with him.

STAGE
Before words

LEARNING OPPORTUNITIES
- To seek out eye contact and respond with smiles to adult attention
- To respond to own name by looking.

YOU WILL NEED
A large, shallow cardboard box; soft cushions and blankets (warm from a radiator or tumble drier); crinkly soft toys or bricks with squeakers for exploring.

Build a nest

Sharing the game

- Line the cardboard box with one of the blankets, then place the warm blankets and cushions into the box. Hide two or three of the soft toys in the nest that you have built.
- Encourage your baby to explore the nest, feeling the warmth of the blankets, and to investigate the different textures and sounds made by the toys.
- Sit on the floor so that you are at the same level as your baby. Find one of the toys in the nest, keep it covered by a blanket, then gently call your baby's name. When she looks to you, say her name, then pull the hidden toy from the blanket and offer it to her.
- If your baby does not look at you when you call her name, pause as she may need a few moments to respond, then call her name again and gently stroke her cheek to gain her attention. When she looks at you, smile in response to her glance, say her name again, then show her the hidden toy.

Taking it further

- Invite a friend and her baby to share the game and explore the nest with you and your baby.
- Play 'Peek-a-boo' with each of the babies in turn. Encourage them to be aware of each other, perhaps by helping them to both pat a toy together, or pass a toy or cushion to each other.

FRIENDS TOGETHER

STAGE
Before words

LEARNING OPPORTUNITIES
- To reach for and give an object
- To smile and reach for a reflection in a mirror.

YOU WILL NEED
A small safety mirror; rug; two or three friends and their babies.

Pass the mirror

Sharing the game

- Sit on the rug with your baby sitting in front of you, facing forwards. Invite your friends and their babies to join you, making a small circle with the babies facing into the centre of the circle.
- Give the mirror to your baby so that he can hold it with two hands. Help him to discover his own reflection. Look at him through the mirror, smiling and saying 'hello'. Encourage him to reach for and pat the mirror image.
- While your child is holding the mirror and trying to look at his reflection, join with your friends to sing this song to a tune that you are familiar with:

  Let's say 'hello' to (*baby's name*), hello, hello.
  Let's say 'hello' to (*baby's name*), hello, hello.
  Hello, (*baby's name*).

- Next, help your baby to pass the mirror into the outstretched hand of the friend who is sitting next to you. As you pass the mirror, sing:

  Pass the mirror round,
  Wait for the song,
  Look! I can see you.
- When your baby has released the mirror into your friend's outstretched hand, your friend can offer it to her own baby and continue the game with the 'Hello' song.

Taking it further

- Use the 'Hello' song with your baby to encourage looking and smiles throughout the day.
- Prompt your baby to reach for offered objects or toys and to release objects into your outstretched hand.

STAGE
Before words

LEARNING OPPORTUNITY
- To shake a toy and share the pleasure with other babies and familiar adults.

YOU WILL NEED
A large plastic hoop with bells and squeakers securely attached; two or three friends and their babies.

Round and round

Sharing the game

- Sit on the floor with your baby facing forwards. Invite your friends and their babies to join you. Encourage and help the babies to share holding the hoop together.

- Play a game of 'Ready, steady, go'. On the word 'go', help the babies to lift the hoop as high as they can, saying, 'Up, up, up', and then lower it together saying, 'Down, down, down'.
- Repeat this a few times, saying, 'Up, up, up' and 'Down, down, down'.
- Next, help the babies to pass the hoop around from hand to hand, singing this song to the tune of 'Here We Go Round the Mulberry Bush' (Traditional) or any other tune that you are comfortable with:

This is the way we go round and round,
Round and round, round and round;
This is the way we go round and round,
Round and round, round and round,
and STOP.

Taking it further

- Place a balloon on a blanket. Hold the edges of the blanket with your baby, your friends and their babies, and bounce the balloon gently up and down as you play the game together.

FRIENDS TOGETHER

STAGE
Before words

LEARNING OPPORTUNITIES
- To take part in a simple game
- To say own name and names of friends.

YOU WILL NEED
A balloon; bag or pillowcase filled with small soft toys; tape recorder; music tape; two or three friends and their children.

THINK FIRST!
Never leave your child unattended with a balloon. The 'pop' noise that the balloon makes as it bursts may distress your child. Remember that burst balloons are a choking hazard.

Balloon antics

Sharing the game

- Sit the children in a circle, with each parent sitting behind their child. Blow up the balloon and place the bag of small soft toys in the middle of the circle.
- Help the children to pass the balloon around the circle as the music plays. When the music stops, lift the balloon up to hide the face of the child that is holding it and sing this song to the tune of 'Frère Jacques' (Traditional), or any other tune that you are comfortable with:

  Where is (*child's name*), where is (*child's name*),
  Peek-a-boo, peek-a-boo,
  Hello (*child's name*), hello (*child's name*)
  Hello you! Hello you!
- Invite the child to choose who they would like to give the balloon to and then to collect a soft toy from the bag to place in their lap.
- Restart the music tape and continue playing the game. Encourage the children to hold out two hands to receive the balloon, and to gently pass it on to the child next to them.
- Using a soft toy as a reward will help the children to stay focused on the game. Do not make the toys too exciting and encourage each child to give the toy a hug, then place it either in their lap or in that of the child next to them.

Taking it further

- Repeat this balloon game with a beach ball. Encourage the children to roll the ball to each other around the circle, instead of passing the balloon.

FRIENDS TOGETHER

STAGE
First words

LEARNING OPPORTUNITIES
- To play co-operatively with another child
- To join in a familiar song.

YOU WILL NEED
A large blue sheet; child's picnic box; hat; cup; plastic fish or picture of a fish drawn on card and cut out; friend and her child.

My big blue boat

Sharing the game

- Spread the blue sheet out on the floor to create the sea. Hold the corners and show the children how to make waves by raising and lowering the corners of the sheet.
- Sit on the sheet facing your child, holding both of her hands with outstretched arms, and rock gently from side to side. Ask your friend to create the waves. Sing the song 'I Love to Row in My Big Blue Boat' (from *Playtime Tunes for Nursery School* by Marion Anderson):

  I love to row in my big blue boat,
  My big blue boat, my big blue boat;
  I love to row in my big blue boat,
  Out on the deep blue sea.

- Play the game again with both of the children sitting on the sheet and pretending to be on the boat. Sing again as you gently help them to hold hands and sway from side to side.

- As the children begin to be able to do this together, invite each child to choose an item to take with them on the boat. Help them to make their choice and let you know by using words or pointing to the item that they would like to take on the boat.
- Sing the song again, making the waves with the sheet and encouraging the children to sway gently from side to side. Stop suddenly in the middle of the song and pause for the children to complete the line, before continuing.

Taking it further

- Make some paper boats for your child and let her play with them in the sink or at bathtime.

FRIENDS TOGETHER

STAGE
First words

LEARNING OPPORTUNITIES
- To use first words to name familiar objects
- To match an object with another of the same.

YOU WILL NEED
A shoebox; old wrapping paper or newspaper; two each of a selection of familiar objects such as toy cars, books, spoons, cups, keys and socks; tape recorder; music tape; two or three of your child's friends.

All wrapped up

Sharing the game

- Place one of each pair of objects into the shoebox. With the rest of the objects, make a large parcel by wrapping one of the objects in the centre, then adding another object with each new layer of paper, as in the traditional game of 'Pass the parcel'.

- Help the children to sit in a circle, then start the music. Play a variation on the 'Pass the parcel' game. When the music stops, invite the child who has the parcel to unwrap a layer to find their object. Encourage them to tell you what they have found, then challenge them to find a matching object from the shoebox.
- Continue playing until all the objects have been found and all the pairs have been made. As well as naming the objects, talk about their use, for example, 'Look, here is the sock, it keeps our feet warm', as you pretend to put the sock on your foot.
- Use the word 'same' to emphasise the matching of objects.

Taking it further

- Play this game with cards from a 'Matching pairs' game.
- Use the pictures from a 'Lotto' game in the layers of the parcel. As each picture is unwrapped, help the children to match it to their 'Lotto' board.

FRIENDS TOGETHER

STAGE
First words

LEARNING OPPORTUNITIES
- To use words to name clothes
- To identify body parts on a doll or teddy.

YOU WILL NEED
Two dolls or teddies; selection of dolls' and children's clothes; one of your child's friends.

Get dressed, Dolly!

Sharing the game

- Sit on the floor with your child and her friend. Spread out all the dolls' and children's clothes on the floor between you.
- Talk with the children about the clothes. Explain that dolls wear some of the clothes and children wear the others. Discuss when the different clothes would be worn, for example, say, 'Look, a coat to keep Dolly warm', 'I've found a sun-hat for you to wear on a hot day' and so on.
- Help the children to make two piles of clothes – one for Dolly and one of children's clothes. Put the children's clothes to one side.
- Give your child and her friend a doll or teddy to dress. Let them take turns to find an item of clothing for it. Ask them to find the item of clothing by name, for example, 'Can you find Teddy some socks?', by where it is worn, for example, 'What will Dolly wear on her head?', or by its use, for example, 'It is very cold today, what will Teddy need to wear to keep warm?'.

- Encourage the children to name body parts on the doll or teddy and then to find the same on you, themselves or each other.

Taking it further

- Give the children a wide variety of dressing-up clothes and help them to choose what they would like to wear for a sunny day, a rainy day, to go to bed, to go swimming and so on.

FRIENDS TOGETHER

STAGE
Putting words together

LEARNING OPPORTUNITIES
- To play co-operatively with another child
- To identify and name body parts on another.

YOU WILL NEED
Two large sheets of paper; felt-tipped pens; glue stick; shiny or colourful scrap pieces of paper; scrap pieces of fabric; wool; string; large buttons or large bottle tops; one of your child's friends.

All about me

Sharing the game

- Invite your child to lie down on the sheet of paper and help his friend to draw around your child to make an outline. As he draws, talk about body parts, for example, 'Look, two little eyes to see with', 'Two big feet to run and jump' and so on.
- When the outline is complete, help the children to work together to add features such as eyes, ears, hair and so on, using the glue and collage scraps.

- Encourage the children to continue decorating the outline by asking questions and commenting, for example, 'What sort of shoes should we make?' or 'What colour hair shall we give him?'.
- Let the children work alongside each other, wherever possible working together. Encourage turn-taking and helping. Provide just one glue stick so that they have to wait a moment for their turn to use it.
- When the outline is complete, make sure that you let the other child have a turn at being drawn around.

Taking it further

- Draw around hands and feet to make outlines to decorate with paint or by sticking on collage pieces.
- Draw around a doll, then place clothes on the outline before dressing her.

FRIENDS TOGETHER

STAGE

Putting words together

LEARNING OPPORTUNITIES

- Use some words to describe feelings
- Listen to other children for a few moments.

YOU WILL NEED

A collection of familiar books, including picture books, story-books, poems, rhymes and information books; three or four large envelopes or paper bags; pencils; two or three of your child's friends.

My favourite book

Sharing the game

- Spend some time enjoying and sharing some of the books with the children. Spread the books on the floor or table and talk together about things that you like in the books, such as favourite characters, pictures, stories or funny rhymes.
- Tell the children about the books that you read when you were a child and when you were read to, such as a favourite bedtime story-book. Help the children to take it in turns to talk to you and discourage them from interrupting each other.
- Explain to the children that you are going to find your favourite book from the ones in the collection, then you are going to put it in a paper bag. Invite the children to do the same. Help each child to attempt to write their name on their envelope or paper bag.
- Gather all the bags together and help the children to sit in a circle. Look at each bag in turn and comment on the book that has been chosen. Some children might want to tell you why they like a book or why they chose it.
- Talk about the characters in the story-books and comment on how they appear in the pictures, for example, 'Look, the baby is crying – he looks sad'. Encourage the children to remark on this, for example, 'Aah, he wanted his mummy' or 'I wonder why he felt sad'.

Taking it further

- Look at picture books with your child and talk about the faces and the emotions using words such as 'happy', 'angry', 'sleepy', 'laughing' and so on.

FRIENDS TOGETHER

STAGE
Putting words together

LEARNING OPPORTUNITIES

- To take on tasks in role-play
- To play alongside another child.

YOU WILL NEED
Dolls; washable dolls' clothes; bowl of warm, bubbly water; bowl of clear water; washing line; clothes pegs; one of your child's friends.

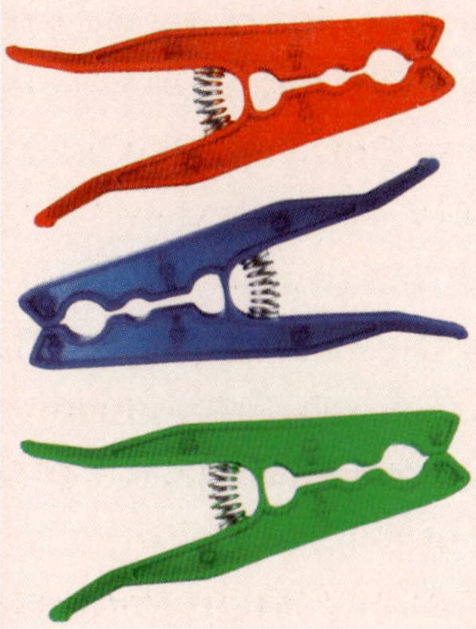

Scrub-a-dub

Sharing the game

- Play this game outdoors.
- Help your child and his friend to undress the dolls. Encourage them to take turns to wash an item of clothing and wring out the suds.
- Encourage the children to take turns to wash the clothes, then to pass them to the other child to be rinsed in the clean water.

- When the clothes are rinsed, encourage the children to take it in turns to wring them.
- Decide with the children whose job it will be to pass the pegs and whose job it will be to peg out the washing. Help them to work this out by saying, 'First it is (*child's name*)'s turn with the pegs, then it is your turn'.
- Involve both your child and his friend as far as possible in the decision making.

Taking it further

- Make up simple rhymes for your child and his friend as they play, such as:

  Scrub-a-dub, Dolly's clothes in the tub
  How shall we get them clean?
  Scrub-a-dub, Dolly's clothes in the tub
  How shall we get them clean?

STAGE
Putting words together

LEARNING OPPORTUNITIES
- To share food and familiar objects with another child
- To make choices.

YOU WILL NEED
A large cardboard box; marker pen; child's toy tea set, including a kettle or teapot; bread and sandwich filling; two types of fruit; cups; jug of water or juice; two of your child's friends.

Polly's picnic

Sharing the game

- Using the pen, mark the outline of a hob and oven on the cardboard box. With your child, make some tiny sandwiches and cut up the fruit into small pieces.
- Invite your child's friends to 'Polly's picnic'.
- Sing this traditional song and help your child to put the toy kettle on and off the pretend stove:

Polly put the kettle on,
Polly put the kettle on,
Polly put the kettle on,
Let's all have tea.
Sukie take it off again,
Sukie take it off again,
Sukie take it off again,
They have all gone away.

- Invite one of your child's friends to offer around the sandwiches. Encourage her to let each child, in turn, have a choice of sandwich. Model the correct words and ask each child to wait their turn and to say 'please' and 'thank you'.

- Let each child have a turn to offer a choice of drinks or the two types of fruit to each of the other children. Emphasise taking turns and let everyone have a choice. Watch to see if your child is making a real choice or simply always asking for the last item offered as part of the choice.

Taking it further

- Give your child choices during your daily routine. Offer real choices and respect your child's decision. Limited choices work best, so, for example, instead of asking, 'What would you like to wear today?', show your child two tops and ask, 'Would you like to wear the blue top or the red top today?'.

CHAPTER 7

Early language and literacy skills are needed if a child is to be a confident communicator as well as able to read well and write effectively. Developing early literacy skills starts within the first few months of life. It is a natural process of emerging skills and enjoyment in stories, books, pictures and magazines, as well as in making marks. Your baby's first mark-making may be creating patterns with his fingers or spoon in his dinner, and will quickly grow to mark-making on paper with crayons, or perhaps with a stick in a puddle, or finger patterns in sand. This chapter provides ideas on how to use and enjoy books and pictures with your baby and young child.

BUSY WITH BOOKS

BOOKS AND BABIES

It is never too early to start sharing books with your baby. She will associate your voice with warmth and security, and this positive feeling will bring enjoyment to her as you read to her. Your baby will associate with being held during pleasurable stories and rhymes, and will learn to listen and later share your enjoyment and attention on the book. Sharing stories, looking at pictures and singing rhymes are all great ways to encourage your baby's early language skills.

How you can help

- Try to read with your baby every day.
- Make it a pleasurable and unhurried time, in a warm and comfortable place.
- Choose books that you can both enjoy. Look for bright colours, textures and a range of picture books, rhyming books and photo books, as well as cloth and board books.
- Very young babies focus best on images held approximately 23cm away. Choose interesting pictures with a strong contrast of colours and support your baby's head well.

CHOOSING BOOKS FOR YOUNG CHILDREN

There is an amazing array of picture books and story-books available for young children, and choosing the best books for your child can be a daunting experience. The value of reading every day with your child, and having a wide selection of books available for your shared enjoyment, is undisputed. Short stories are best. Pictures should be clear, however children enjoy a wide variety of styles of illustration, so be guided more by the content than the pictures. Look for books with rhythm, rhyme and repetition. Older babies and very small children particularly enjoy photograph books and pictures of other babies.

Use books with textures, touch-and-feel books and books with holes for little fingers. Lift-the-flap books are always popular and hold very young children's attention well. Try to get a good variety of styles of books, including poetry books, information

books and collections of stories and rhymes, as well as individual story-books. Concept books, for example, about shapes and colours, also provide useful experiences.

How you can help

- Share a wide variety of books, stories and pictures with your child.
- Let your child see you using and enjoying books and magazines.
- Read every day to your child and occasionally, let your child choose the book for your to read.
- Keep the books where your child can easily get at them.
- Take books with you when you go out, and give your child a book to look at on journeys.

LITERACY FOR EVERY DAY

Children learn by imitation, and if they see you enjoying and using books and writing at home, then they will be keen to join in or copy you. Your child needs to have the chance to use and enjoy mark-making as well as looking at books and pictures in everyday situations, at home and out and about. This way, he will learn the importance and value of mark-making, that it has purpose and that it can be useful as well as enjoyed. Have materials for mark-making frequently available to help your child's writing skills. As well as making marks on blank paper, your child will enjoy using cards, magazines and junk mail. Keep felt-tipped pens and crayons close to hand for your child to use.

How you can help

- Let your child make marks as you write letters, lists and so on.
- Invite your child to help you make his own shopping list or to 'write' lists of other things.
- Write messages for other family members and let your child deliver them.
- Encourage him to add his own marks to 'sign' birthday cards and invitations.

THE JOY OF READING

If your child sees you reading for pleasure and information, she will begin to understand the value of books. Letting your child see you using printed material in everyday situations will help her to recognise the range of purposes for which we use print. Make the most of opportunities at home and as you go out and about.

How you can help

- Read aloud important signs that you see, such as 'Exit' or 'No parking', and talk about what they mean.
- Look at instructions with your child.
- Let your child help you to open letters and parcels.
- Give your child the shopping list to hold when you are shopping.
- Look at pictures in magazines together.
- Look at the television guide together.
- Pick up information leaflets and look at them with your child.
- Stop to read notice-boards together.

STAGE
Before words

LEARNING OPPORTUNITIES
- To focus on a pattern
- To smile in response to attention.

YOU WILL NEED
A piece of black A5 paper; piece of white A5 card; glue; scissors; baby's chair.

Black and white

Sharing the game

- Cut strips of black paper and glue them on to the piece of white card to make a black and white striped pattern on one side of the card.
- Cut the remaining black paper into small squares and glue these on to the reverse of the white card in a chequerboard pattern.
- Tilt your baby's chair so that his head is well supported. Sit on the floor next to your child's chair so that you can lean over to be close to his face.
- Hold the card approximately 23cm from your baby's face. (In the first few months, this is the distance at which your baby can see most clearly.) Smile and talk to your baby as he gazes at the card.
- If necessary, tap the back of the card gently with your finger to draw your baby's attention to the picture.
- After a few minutes, turn over the card for your baby to look at a different pattern. Young babies find black and white patterns particularly interesting and will watch the card as you move it slowly, up and down, and side to side.

Taking it further

- Make a book of black and white picture cards and share it with your baby.
- Attach some black and white striped shapes securely to a mobile, and hang it in your baby's room.

BUSY WITH BOOKS

STAGE
Before words

LEARNING OPPORTUNITIES
- To look at a picture for a few moments
- To learn about the use of familiar objects.

YOU WILL NEED
Four pieces of A5 card; pens; fabric and card offcuts; glue; scissors.

Touch and feel

Sharing the game

- Draw an outline of a shoe, cup, brush and spoon, one on each piece of card.
- Use the fabric and paper offcuts to fill in the shapes, for example, smooth, bright or shiny paper for the spoon, a spiky texture for the brush and so on. Ensure that each completed shape is similar in colour and texture to the object, and is familiar to your baby.

- Sit with your baby on your knee and, together, explore the cards one at a time. Encourage her to feel the shape and to focus on the card as you say the appropriate object word, for example, 'Cup', then '(*Your baby's name*), look, cup'. Use simple language and focus on the object word, then pretend to drink from a cup, saying, 'Look, cup'.
- Sing the following song to the tune of 'Here We Go Round the Mulberry Bush' (Traditional) or another tune that you are comfortable with:

This is the way we drink from a cup,
Drink from a cup, drink from a cup,
This is the way we drink from a cup,
Drink, drink, drink.

- Continue to play the game, giving your baby plenty of time to explore and feel the cards. Change the words of the song to fit with each object, for example, 'This is the way we brush our hair', 'This is the way we lick the spoon', and 'This is the way we put on our shoes'.

Taking it further

- Give your baby real objects to hold as you sing the song.
- Make more cards, for example, objects in a favourite song or rhyme, such as 'Twinkle, Twinkle, Little Star' or 'Humpty Dumpty' (both Traditional).

BUSY WITH BOOKS

STAGE
Before words

LEARNING OPPORTUNITIES
- To use a pointing gesture
- To find familiar objects and pictures of familiar objects on request.

YOU WILL NEED
A shoebox filled with familiar objects, such as a toy car, ball, book, keys, shoe and hat; set of picture cards of these objects.

Matching muddles

Sharing the game

- Sit opposite your baby so that your faces are at the same level. Give him the objects, one at a time, to explore, then place them in the shoebox.
- When your baby has had a chance to explore all the objects, put the shoebox to one side. Give him one of the picture cards and encourage him to copy you as you name the object that it shows. Try to avoid asking your baby directly what the object is, but share his interest in the card and say, 'Wow, look at that, it's a…', then pause for him to attempt the appropriate word, or, if necessary, for you to name the picture.
- Give your baby the shoebox as you hold the picture up for him to see. Ask, 'Can you find the ball?'. Help him to look through the objects in the shoebox and find the ball.
- Focus on the object word rather than on the picture, but mention that they are the same.

- Continue playing and after a few more turns, put two or three picture cards out for your baby. Ask him to find you one of the pictures. Help him to point to the named picture, then to find the object in the shoebox.

Taking it further

- Play the game with just the pictures. Ask your baby to find a named picture from a choice of three, then help him to find the named object from the place that it is usually kept in at home. For example, encourage your child to take you into the kitchen and point to where the spoons are kept, or to find the ball from the toy-box.

STAGE
Before words

LEARNING OPPORTUNITIES
- To point to pictures of familiar people and attempt to name them
- To share a picture book for a few moments.

YOU WILL NEED
Clear photographs of family members, pets, your house, familiar items such as your baby's pushchair, your car or the bus that you use when you go out; scrapbook; glue; scissors.

My photo album

Sharing the game

- Make a book for your baby, with one photograph on each page. Choose recent, clear photographs, with only one person in each. Put the photographs in a logical order, starting with the immediate family, and then, perhaps, pets and your home. Follow this with a photograph of your car or the bus, and a photograph of other people to whom your baby is close, such as grandparents or very good friends. Make the book as robust as possible so that your baby can, in time, look at it on her own and enjoy handling her first photo album.
- Sit with your baby and help her to turn the pages. Use a pointing gesture and a gentle tap on the photograph to draw your baby's attention to each page. Name the people and comment about what they are doing, using an action word with their name, for example, 'Look, Daniel's running' or 'Look, Granny's reading'.
- When you reach the photograph of your baby, draw her attention to it not just as 'baby', but say, 'Look it's (*your baby's name*), look it's you!' and take her hand to touch or point to herself.

Taking it further

- Use this photo album as a starting-point to create a family story-book for your baby, with photos of events that are of particular importance to her, for example, her first steps, her first day at nursery, her first sports day and so on.

STAGE
First words

LEARNING OPPORTUNITIES
- To name and find familiar objects
- To share a story-book for a few minutes.

YOU WILL NEED
A familiar picture book, such as *Where's Spot?* by Eric Hill (Puffin Books), or your child's favourite story-book; four or five objects that are named in the story and appear in the pictures; small bag or child's shopping basket.

Bag that story!

Sharing the game

- Sit comfortably with your child and read the story-book to him. Give your child plenty of time to see the pictures and help him to turn the pages.
- When you have read the story, go through the book together and look at the pictures. Talk about the different familiar objects that you can see in each picture.
- Name the objects in the pictures and ask your child to find them, for example, say, 'Where's the ball?', or encourage him to name the objects, by asking, 'What has the baby taken to bed?'.
- If your child is already using some first words to label objects, help him to think about action words by commenting on what the characters in the pictures are doing, for example, 'Look, the dog is swimming', or ask your child, 'Look at the dog, what is he doing?'.
- Return to the first picture in the book and point out one of the objects on the page. Give your child the basket and invite him to find that object.

- Turn the page and help your child to choose another object in the picture that he could add to his basket. Continue to play the game, collecting the familiar objects that your child can see in the pictures.

Taking it further

- Share the book again and when you have read each page, ask your child to find an object from the picture in his basket, for example, 'Can you find the ball?'.

STAGE
First words

LEARNING OPPORTUNITIES
- To use first words and combine words and gestures to mean 'gone'
- To take turns.

YOU WILL NEED
Two shoeboxes; scissors; fabric scraps; glue; set of picture cards.

Picture posting

Sharing the game

- Create a posting-box from each shoebox by cutting a slit into the top, big enough to post the picture cards.
- Give your child and yourself a box each. Help your child to decorate her box by gluing scraps of fabric on to it. Decorate your own box in the same way. Write your child's name on her box and add your name to your box.
- Place three picture cards on the floor and ask your child to find one of the cards, for example, say, 'Where's the ball?'. When she has found the correct card, help her to post it into her box saying, 'In (*your child's name*)'s box, bye-bye ball', then raise your hands, palms upwards, gesturing and saying, 'Gone, ball gone'.

- Take it in turns to find a card and post it. When it is your turn, ask, 'Mummy's box or (*your child's name*)'s box?'. Encourage your child to make choices and use first words. Keep the game consistent, using simple repetitive language such as 'Mummy's turn, or (*your child's name*)'s turn?'.
- Continue playing the game, taking turns to post the picture cards. Help your child to use or imitate two-word phrases where an object word is combined with a word to describe possession, for example, 'Jodie's book'.

Taking it further

- Turn all the cards face-down in a pile and take turns to turn over a card, name the object in the picture and then post it into a box.

BUSY WITH BOOKS

STAGE
First words

LEARNING OPPORTUNITIES
- To recognise and talk about familiar routines
- To name familiar objects.

YOU WILL NEED
Photographs of important times in your child's day, such as waking up, breakfast time, getting dressed, family members leaving for school or work, playing, reading a book, out in the garden, teatime, bathtime and going to bed; pieces of A5 card; glue; clear plastic pockets to protect the photographs.

Make my day

Sharing the game

- Stick each photograph on to a piece of card. Wrap each card securely in a plastic pocket to protect them.
- Share the cards with your child, one at a time. Talk about each card using familiar first words, as well as words to describe how he may have been feeling in each photograph, such as happy, warm, sleepy, excited and so on.
- Let your child handle the photo cards and choose one to share with you. Help him to recognise the order of his day. For example, if he has given you the breakfast-time card, find the getting-dressed card and talk about how this comes next.
- Keep the cards easily available throughout your day and pass your child a card at the appropriate time, for example, give him the bathtime picture to look at as you undress him for his bath. This will help his understanding of familiar routines and also prompt him to talk about the pictures, encouraging his use of words to describe familiar objects.

Taking it further

- At appropriate times during the day, choose one of the photo cards, such as teatime, and ask your child to find familiar objects that are associated with that routine, for example, a spoon, cup, bib and so on.

STAGE
First words

LEARNING OPPORTUNITIES
- To recognise pictures of familiar objects
- To look at photos, pictures and line drawings.

YOU WILL NEED
A small square box; pen; scissors; glue; six pictures of familiar objects such as a teddy, hat, shoe, ball and so on, including two photographs, two pictures cut from a magazine or brochure, and two simple line drawings; six matching objects; shoebox or pillowcase.

First word dice

Sharing the game

- Stick a picture on to each of the sides of the small square box to create a dice.
- Place the matching objects into the shoebox or pillowcase.
- Help your child to throw the dice.
- Hold the dice so that you cover all the pictures except for the one facing up. Say to your child, 'Look, you have the ball', then ask her to find the matching object from the shoebox.
- Continue playing, asking your child to identify the picture on the dice, then match it to the object in the shoebox.

Taking it further

- Change the pictures to include a wider variety of first words and action words. For example, if you throw the dice to show a picture of a baby crawling, then crawl around the room with your child.
- Share a wide range of picture books with your child. Visit your local library and look for photograph books, lift-the-flap books and picture books.

STAGE
Putting words together

LEARNING OPPORTUNITIES
- To use action words and object words together
- To understand and use the words 'big' and 'little'.

YOU WILL NEED
Six sheets of A4 card; glue; old catalogues; scissors; glue; small bag.

Lift the flap

Sharing the game

- Cut each sheet of card into four equal rectangles. Take 12 rectangles and fold them across the short edge, approximately two centimetres from the top. Pair each of the cards with the folded tops with a flat piece of card and glue them together along the top. This will make a flap that can be lifted to see the other piece of card underneath. You will now have 12 'lift-the-flap' cards.
- Help your child to choose pictures from the catalogues to go under each flap. Encourage him to select pictures showing actions, such as a child bouncing a ball or a girl laughing, as well as some pictures of familiar objects. Look for objects where you can describe them as big or little, or pairs of big and little objects, such as an adult's shoe and a baby's shoe. Cut and stick one picture under the flap of each card.
- Put the cards into the bag and invite your child to take them out one at a time. Ask him to lift the flap and to describe the picture for you to guess what it is. Prompt him with questions, or by offering choices such as, 'Is it something to wear?' or 'Is it something to play with?'.
- If your child names the object, encourage him to use two- and three-word phrases, for example, ask him what colour the object is and, if it is a car, whether it is a big car or a small car.
- Finally, let your child reveal to you the surprise picture under the flap. Enjoy the moment together and praise your child for playing the game so well.

Taking it further

- Look at the cards together, then carefully write a label under each picture, for example, 'a red car' or 'a big dog'. Read the writing to your child as you are doing this.
- Let your child decorate the front of each card with a variety of coloured pens and crayons.

BUSY WITH BOOKS

STAGE
Putting words together

LEARNING OPPORTUNITIES
- To make marks intentionally
- To understand that writing can convey meaning.

YOU WILL NEED
Old envelopes; old birthday cards; stickers; selection of pens and paper; scissors; bag; large cardboard box.

Making my mark

Sharing the game

- Cut a slit in the cardboard box to make a post-box, and a flap at the back of the box for emptying.
- Gather together the birthday cards and take it in turn with your child to post them in the box. Tell your child who each card that you are posting is for, naming family and friends that are familiar to your child. Ask her to tell you who she is sending her cards to.
- Empty the post-box and put all the cards into the bag.
- Sit with your child and encourage her to find an envelope for each birthday card. Write inside each card the name of the person that she wants to send it to. Then pass the card to her and invite her to add her own marks.

- Together, place each card in an envelope and add a sticker for a stamp. Your child may choose to draw on the front of the envelope. Write alongside your child, making up addresses for each envelope.
- Allow your child the freedom to make marks and to scribble on the cards and envelopes. Respect her efforts and try at this stage not to attribute meaning to any of the shapes or marks that you see. It is important at this stage that your child enjoy making marks and begin to understand that writing and text can carry meaning and have purpose.

Taking it further

- Create a post office for your child to play with, by adding some small boxes and parcels, and stickers for stamps. Give her small books and pens for her to make notes.

STAGE
Putting words together

LEARNING OPPORTUNITIES
- To match objects and pictures
- To see that words and pictures convey meaning and have a purpose.

YOU WILL NEED
A supermarket brochure showing food items; scissors; glue; piece of paper; pens.

The shopping list

Sharing the game

- Play this game with your child before going shopping.
- Sit with your child and write a short shopping list of five or six food items. Write slowly and carefully, using lower-case letters. Give your child a piece of paper so he can write his own shopping list, too.
- Look through the supermarket brochure together and find the items on your shopping list.
- Help your child to cut out the pictures and stick them on the shopping list next to the appropriate words.
- Ask your child to draw any items that are on the shopping list that you cannot find matching pictures for.
- Take the shopping list with you when you go shopping and help your child to find each item. Ask him to tell you what you need next by looking at the pictures on the shopping list.
- When you have finished the shopping, invite your child to check your basket against his list so that you can match each item that you have bought to the shopping list.
- Give your child the receipt. Look at it together and read the items to him.

Taking it further

- Look at different types of print around the shop. Match the words on the shopping list to words on packets and tins.
- Create a role-play shop at home with empty packets and cartons on a coffee table. Include pens and paper for making shopping lists as well as labels and price tags.

BUSY WITH BOOKS

STAGE
Putting words together

LEARNING OPPORTUNITIES
- To match objects to outline shapes
- To practise holding a pen.

YOU WILL NEED
Four sheets of A4 paper; scissors; stapler; pens; leaf; shoe; toy plate; book; spoon.

Match it!

Sharing the game

- Cut each sheet of paper in half, then fold it in half again. Staple together along the fold to make a small book with 16 pages.
- Ask your child to choose one of the objects and place it on the first page of the book. Carefully draw around the outline.
- Continue with the other objects, helping your child to hold a pen and draw around each item to make the outlines.
- Look around the house and outside for more familiar objects to draw around. Draw around each other's hands, too.
- When the book is complete, take it in turns to find the object to match each outline. Talk about the objects, commenting on their colour, shape and texture.
- If you find a leaf to match the outline, encourage your child to find other leaves. Use words to describe the size of the outline and the item, such as 'big' and 'little', as well as relative size such as 'bigger' and 'smaller'.
- Next, find one of the objects for your child and ask her to find the page and outline that it matches. Take turns to play the game.

Taking it further

- Draw some of the outlines of the shapes on to black paper and then on to white paper. Match the outlines to each other as well as to the object.
- Look for pictures of the objects in books and magazines.

STAGE
Putting words together

LEARNING OPPORTUNITIES
- To recognise and match colours
- To use two- and three-word phrases to describe pictures.

YOU WILL NEED
Sheets of red, yellow and blue paper; pens; scissors; small plate to draw around; old catalogues and magazines.

Colourful caterpillars

Sharing the game

- Draw around the plate to make several small red, blue and yellow circles. Cut these out and help your child to sort them according to colour, for example, all the blue ones together and so on.
- Lay each pile of circles together in a line on the floor to make a red caterpillar, a blue caterpillar and a yellow caterpillar. Help your child to draw a face on the first circle of each caterpillar.
- Ask your child to find red toys, and other small items from around the home that are red, and place one on each of the red circles on the red caterpillar.

- Look through the magazines together and find pictures to cut out to place on the circles, such as red shoes or a red car.
- Talk about each object that you find. Encourage your child to use two- and three-word phrases, and to include words that name the colour, such as 'the blue bike', 'the boy is wearing a yellow hat' and so on.

Taking it further

- Make multicoloured caterpillars by mixing red, blue and yellow circles. Take it in turns with your child to find an object or a picture to match the caterpillar circles.
- Make stripy caterpillars, using just two colours and making a pattern, for example, red, blue, red blue.
- Give your child an object, such as a red ball, and ask him to choose where to place it on the caterpillar.

STAGE
Putting words together

LEARNING OPPORTUNITIES
- To sort objects by colour
- To recognise and use colour words as part of two-word phrases.

YOU WILL NEED
A large sheet of thick white paper; red, blue, yellow and green felt-tipped pens; scissors; glue; coloured ribbon; selection of old magazines and catalogues; fabric scraps.

Rainbow kite

Sharing the game

- Cut a large diamond shape to create a kite from the sheet of paper. Using the felt-tipped pens, draw lines across the diamond to make four triangle shapes. Outline each triangle with a different colour so that you have a red, blue, yellow and green section on your kite.
- Show your child the kite that you are making, and ask her to help you to find pictures to add to the kite. Look together through the magazines for red pictures for the red section of the kite and so on. Encourage your child to turn the pages of the magazines looking for red objects, then help her to cut and paste them on to the kite.

- Encourage your child to use two- and three-word phrases including the colour of the object, such as 'yellow flower', 'dirty red boots' and so on. Cut out a number of objects of the different colours and help your child to sort and stick them on the kite, matching and naming colours as she does so.
- Decorate the kite further by sticking scraps of fabric on to the different coloured sections. Invite your child to write and draw on the kite, too.
- Attach the ribbon to the kite and encourage your child to mark her name on the ribbon.
- Share your child's enjoyment of the kite trailing behind her as she runs around.

Taking it further

- Make other kites by sorting the pictures into four groups of food, clothes, vehicles and toys.

CHAPTER 8

Spending just a couple of minutes every day on a one-to-one basis with your baby and young child is a great opportunity to make a real difference to her early language skills. One of the essential elements of effective communication is 'shared attention'. This is the common interest that two people share when they are communicating, using words, facial expression, gesture or body language. It is the moment when your baby responds to your approaches and begins to communicate with you and share pleasure and interest in the exchange. Make the most of this precious time with your baby and young child by playing the games in this chapter.

JUST THE TWO OF US

FIRST ATTENTION

In the first few months of his life, your baby will show an intense interest in the faces of familiar people and recognise and respond to the voices of those around him. He will show an awareness of environmental sounds and may be startled or distressed by sudden or unfamiliar noises, such as a door banging. Your baby will enjoy looking at you and exploring your face. He will focus best on faces and objects that are held approximately 23cm away from him. You will be his favourite plaything, as he enjoys touching, tickling and stroking, finger play and songs. He will enjoy exploring your face and will imitate your facial expressions. 'Peek-a-boo' and other early gentle surprise and tickling games, such as 'Round and round the garden like a teddy bear', all provide great opportunities for your baby to enjoy and respond to you, building shared attention and practising many of the earliest language skills.

How you can help

- Support your baby's head well during these special moments of play and interaction. He will be able to focus on you and the game, rather than having to concentrate on holding his head up.
- Sing and talk to your baby at every opportunity, but especially at the end of each care routine, such as changing nappies or bathtime, when you can have enjoy a cuddle and some finger-rhyme play or tickling games.

INTERACTING WITH YOUR TODDLER

Older babies and toddlers can be very single-minded and determined. Although they enjoy your attention, some parents may feel that for their young child, this attention is very much on their child's terms. This is an entirely appropriate and ordinary stage in every child's development, but it does not make it any easier to find ways of enjoying a few moments of relaxed play together. Your young child may be very determined to play and interact with your on her own terms. She is busy exploring her world and has discovered the power that she has to have an effect on it, and most significantly, to try out this effect on those most important to her and whom she can trust. There is a lot that you can do to make any special one-to-one time with your toddler more enjoyable and purposeful.

How you can help

- Let your child take the lead in the game, by offering choices and using her particular interests.
- Choose your moment carefully, when your child is calm, not too tired or hungry and is seeking your attention.
- Try not to interrupt your child's play. Young children can become very absorbed in their toys and games and will be more open to your suggestions and attentions when they have finished with their activity.
- Turn off the television and put away some of the toys and distractions. Sometimes, just sit and have a quiet cuddle for a few minutes before playing with your child. Get into the habit of having some quiet one-to-one time for a few moments every day. Young children like routine and your child will soon begin to anticipate this time.

HAVING FUN WITH LANGUAGE

Appealing to children's sense of humour and fun is a great way to gain and keep their attention on activities. Playing with words and making up nonsense rhymes are important in your child's emerging language skills. Elements of surprise and wonderment are all great tools when engaging your child. A few moments of uninterrupted time with no distractions should be rewarding for both of you.

How you can help

- Try to be fun, flexible and spontaneous. Look for opportunities in everyday life to explore words by playing interaction games and songs.
- Make tickling games, 'Peek-a-boo' and nursery rhymes part of your familiar routines.
- Play with your child as you help him to get washed or dressed.

LISTENING TO YOUR CHILD

One-to-one time is a good opportunity to listen carefully to how your child uses language. As she starts to use more words and becomes conversational, you will begin to see that she uses language for a whole range of purposes. For example, asking for what she wants or needs, telling you what is happening, what has happened in the past or predicting ahead to what might happen in the future, and to reason with you. She will use language to tell you how she feels and, in time, how other people feel. She will ask questions, make comments and begin to tease you, as well as use it for humour and fun.

How you can help

- Listen carefully to your child. Try not to interrupt and give her plenty of time to finish.
- Help your child by asking questions that need more than just 'yes' or 'no' for an answer.
- Use some of your child's own words in your reply and encourage her to carry on. Try to stop what you are doing and get down to her eye level, so that she can see that you are listening and that what she has to say is important to you.

STAGE
Before words

LEARNING OPPORTUNITIES
- To repeat own sounds
- To make sounds to gain attention.

YOU WILL NEED
A warm rug or blanket; your baby's favourite soft toy; warm, dry flannel; dry sponge.

Tickle on the tum

Sharing the game

- Place your baby on the rug or blanket. Sing or talk to him, gently stroking and touching his cheek, arms and tummy. Watch to see where he prefers to be stroked and gently tickled.
- Show your baby his favourite soft toy, then place it quickly behind your back and, with an animated voice, say, 'Gone, where's it gone?'. Smile and wait for your baby to make a sound or to glance towards the hidden toy, then gently and slowly bring the toy to the front, saying, 'Here it is!'.
- Move the toy towards your baby and tickle him gently with the toy. Build the anticipation of the tickle with smiles, looking into your baby's eyes, and say, 'It's coming'. Give the toy to your baby to hold and hug. When he is ready, hold out an outstretched hand and gently take the toy from your baby, helping him to put it in your hand.

- Repeat the game with the warm flannel and the dry sponge. Each time, encourage your baby to look for or vocalise for the hidden object. Give him plenty of time to explore the textures of the objects.
- If your baby makes sounds of excitement in response to your attention, copy his sounds back, imitating them carefully, and enjoy some turn-taking baby talk. Stay close to your baby and reinforce your pleasure at his sounds with tickles and attention.

Taking it further

- Play this game with a wide range of suitable objects of different textures.
- Look out for soft fabric books and touch-and-feel picture books at your local library.

JUST THE TWO OF US

STAGE
Before words

LEARNING OPPORTUNITIES
- To copy as you clap hands
- To copy sound patterns.

YOU WILL NEED
A small sheet of bubble wrap; chiffon scarf; thick wool; fluffy or furry fabric.

Clap hands!

Sharing the game

- Sit opposite your baby, so that your faces are at the same level.
- Begin by playing 'Pat-a-cake' with your baby. Next hold her hands between yours so that when you clap your hands, her hands are brought together, too. Clap your hands together to match the beat of this rhyme, saying a word with each clap:

  Clap, clap, clap hands, clippety, clippety, clap
  Clap, clap, clap hands, clippety, clippety, clap.
- When you have said the rhyme, ask your baby, 'Again?' and wait for her to make a sound or attempt to copy your sound, before starting again. Repeat any sound that your baby makes in response to 'Again?'. Show your pleasure with smiles and repeat her sound back to her.

- Give your baby the fluffy fabric to hold and feel. Then lay the fabric over your hands like a cloth and play the clapping game, clapping your baby's hands together gently. This will be a very different sensation for your baby. Stop in the middle of the rhyme and encourage her to vocalise to let you know to continue.
- Play the game again with the bubble wrap. Show your baby your fingers under the bubble wrap and tap it together. Enjoy the feel of the bubble wrap as you play the clapping game.

Taking it further

- Give your baby plenty of opportunities to grasp objects with two hands together in the middle.
- Provide a range of objects for your baby to tap and pat. Give her plenty of uninterrupted time to explore the objects and repeat her favourite songs and rhymes.

STAGE
Before words

LEARNING OPPORTUNITIES
- To use a pointing gesture
- To make a choice.

YOU WILL NEED
A dark hand towel or similar; foil or shiny paper; teddy bear.

Twinkle, little star

Sharing the game

- Cut out two or three stars from the foil.
- Sit on the floor opposite your baby. Offer one of the stars to him, and help him to place it on the towel.
- Encourage your baby to hold the towel with you, stretched out so that the stars can be seen.
- Sing 'Twinkle, Twinkle, Little Star' (Traditional) and at the end of the song, fold the blanket over the stars and gently put it to one side.
- Next, hold the teddy on your knee and sing 'Humpty Dumpty Sat on a Wall' (Traditional), letting the teddy fall to the floor during the rhyme. At the end of the rhyme, pick the teddy up, give him a hug and say, 'Aah'. Offer the teddy to your baby to hug.
- Hold the teddy in one hand and a star in the other. Ask your baby, 'Teddy or stars?'. Encourage your baby to point to the object that he wants. If, for example, he looks towards the star and vocalises, say, 'Star, you want the star'. Give your baby the star to hold for a few moments before prompting him to place it on the towel, then sing 'Twinkle, Twinkle, Little Star' again.
- Each time you play, encourage your baby to indicate his choice with a glance, a pointing gesture, or perhaps by making a sound or attempting the word.

Taking it further

- Make the most of quiet times with your baby and say favourite nursery rhymes or finger rhymes, or play tickling games.

STAGE
Before words

LEARNING OPPORTUNITIES
- To look at own hands
- To smile and vocalise when given attention.

YOU WILL NEED
Shiny buttons; small bells or squeakers; brightly coloured ribbon; black and white ribbon; fine elastic; scissors.

THINK FIRST!
Make sure that everything is attached very securely and never leave your baby unattended with small items.

Look at me

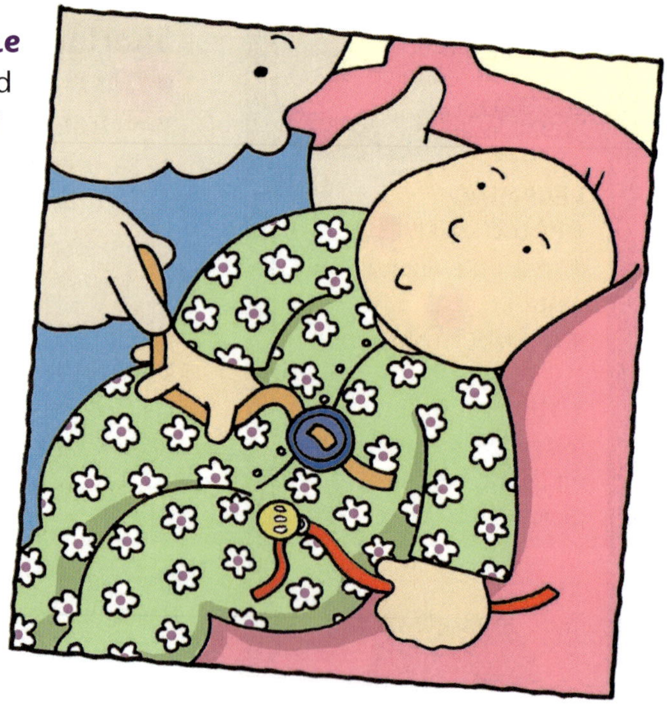

Sharing the game

- Tie the buttons and bells on to lengths of black and white ribbon. Make bracelets with the elastic by threading on buttons and some of the squeakers or bells.
- Sit opposite your baby, with your faces at the same level. Make sure that her head is well supported so that she can focus on looking and smiling, rather than concentrating on holding her head up.
- Wrap the ribbons loosely through your baby's fingers and encourage her to look at them. Pull them gently through her fingers and bring each one up so that it is close to her face. Remember that small babies focus best on objects that are held approximately 23cm away from their faces.
- Shake the ribbons with the bells and press the squeakers to gain your baby's attention before offering the ribbon to her. If you have an older baby, encourage her to reach and grasp for the ribbons, by offering them from the side, to one hand.
- Wrap the ribbons around both wrists and bring your baby's hands together to clap her hands.

Taking it further

- Wrap the ribbons loosely around your hand and your baby's together, then lift your hand and wriggle your fingers so that the ribbon falls.
- Play these games with your baby's toes, too!

JUST THE TWO OF US

STAGE
First words

LEARNING OPPORTUNITIES
- To look up when name is called
- To recognise and name body parts.

YOU WILL NEED
A selection of small stickers.

Happy hands

Sharing the game

- Sit on the floor with your child. Place a sticker on two of your fingers. Walk your fingers towards your child and say, '(*Your child's name*), look who is coming, who is coming to tickle you!'. If your child looks at your face instead of your fingers, tap your fingers gently on the floor so that he is guided towards the noise.
- Walk your fingers gently towards your child, then up his arm, and tickle him on the nose and say, '(*Your child's name*), I'm going to tickle your nose'. Using your child's name first will help him to focus on your words.
- Play again, tickling your child's toes. This time, when you have walked your fingers to his toes, wriggle your fingers very close to his toes and say, '(*Your child's name*), I'm going to tickle your…'. Pause and make a small gasp to prompt him to say or look at his toes. Finish the game by gently tickling and saying, 'Toes'.
- Play the game again, tickling your baby's tummy, hands, ears and hair. Each time, encourage him to name the body part.

Taking it further

- Play the game with finger puppets, or perhaps in the bath with a flannel wrapped around your hand.
- Place one of your hands on the floor and help your child to put his hand on top of yours. Put your other hand on top of his hand, then prompt him to place his hand over yours. Pull your hand gently from the bottom of the stack and place it on the top. Help your child to do the same and continue moving hands from the bottom of the stack to the top.

JUST THE TWO OF US

STAGE
First words

LEARNING OPPORTUNITIES
- To name familiar objects
- To take turns.

YOU WILL NEED
A large box; black paper; dark sheet; scissors; sticky tape; torch; selection of familiar objects such as a spoon, keys, shoe, sock, cup and so on (try to choose shiny, fluorescent or brightly coloured objects).

Shine that torch!

Sharing the game

- Line the box with the black paper. Tape the familiar objects to the sides and in the corners inside the box. Place the box on the floor on its side and spread the dark sheet over the top.
- Give your child the torch and encourage her to find out how it switches on and off. Shine the torch around the room, looking in dark corners and under chairs and sofas or other pieces of furniture.
- Crawl under the dark sheet with your child and let her shine the torch inside the box. Encourage her to name the objects as she finds them.
- Invite your child to shine the torch on a particular object and to name it. Then encourage her to shine the torch on a particular object by describing the object by its use, rather than its name, for example, 'Can you find something that you use to eat your dinner?'.
- Take it in turns to hold the torch to find and name the different objects that are in the box.

Taking it further

- Change the objects in the box to a particular theme, for example, all bathroom objects such as a toothbrush, sponge, bath toy, flannel, and empty shampoo bottle. Also try using objects of the same colour such as all yellow, or all shiny objects.
- Take your child to explore your outdoor environment with a torch, taking it in turns to shine the torch on different objects, and then naming and finding them.

STAGE
First words

LEARNING OPPORTUNITIES
- To hand an object to you when asked
- To name familiar people from their photographs.

YOU WILL NEED
A special box or bag; three objects of special importance to your child, such as a favourite soft toy, a comfort object, birthday card or favourite toy; three objects of special importance to you, such as a piece of jewellery, photograph, key or object belonging to a close family member; photographs of family members.

Special treasure

Sharing the game

- Place all the treasure objects carefully in the special box or bag. Sit with your child and take objects out of the bag one at a time.
- Encourage your child to name the object, then to talk to him, helping him to tell you a little more about the object.
- Talk about how he feels about a particular object and why, for example, say, 'Look, here's your teddy. He is really special, he sleeps in your bed every night', then give the teddy a hug and pass it to your child to hug.
- Make each object special and important. Show your child the jewellery and tell him how precious it is to you. If appropriate, let him try it on or place it on you. Help him to handle the objects carefully and replace them in the bag or put them away safely. Focus on making this a special sharing time, and encourage your child to be gentle and unhurried as he explores the objects with you.

- Look at the photos together. Give your child plenty of time to hold and look at them. Talk about each person and prompt your child to name them – for example, say, 'Look, here is Granny, she lives a long way away' or 'Look, here is baby Drew, see how tiny he is'.

Taking it further

- Take a few moments to let your child try your shoes on, or perhaps put your coat or gloves on. These are special moments that are significant in building your relationship and to show your child that you have the time to listen and enjoy being with him. This time is important as it will give your child the confidence and security that he needs to make good progress with his language skills.

JUST THE TWO OF US

STAGE
First words

LEARNING OPPORTUNITIES
- To imitate actions, sounds and words
- To name more body parts.

YOU WILL NEED
Just yourself and your child.

My body

Sharing the game

- Sit opposite your child so that your faces are at the same level. Tap your feet on the floor and sing this song to the tune of 'Row, Row, Row Your Boat' (Traditional) or one that you are comfortable with:

  Tap, tap, tap your feet,
  Tap your feet like this,
  Tap, tap, tap your feet,
  Tap your feet like this.

- Sing again, encouraging your child to join in, tapping her feet and singing the tune. Pause in the middle of the tune for your child to add the next word.
- Play the game again, choosing different body parts and making a range of sounds and actions, such as patting your knees, wriggling your toes, nodding your head and so on. Combine big movements such as swinging arms, with a loud singing voice, and small actions such as tapping noses, with a whispered song.

- Change the rhyme to help maintain your child's interest. Chant the rhyme 'Jelly on the plate' (Traditional) and make your whole body wobble from side to side. Prompt your child to join in.

  Jelly on the plate, jelly on the plate;
  Wibble-wobble, wibble-wobble,
  Jelly on the plate!

- Play again, changing the words and actions to match your child's favourite foods or interests. For example, raise your arms above your head to make a tall tube and wave from side to side, singing:

  Sweeties in the tube, sweeties in the tube;
  Wiggle-wiggle, wiggle-wiggle,
  Sweeties in the tube!

Taking it further

- Share some finger rhymes with your child and keep a few favourites for special times when there are just the two of you, such as getting dry after a bath, or perhaps just before bed.

JUST THE TWO OF US

STAGE
Putting words together

LEARNING OPPORTUNITIES
- To use describing words
- To count to three with you.

YOU WILL NEED
Wet day; wet-weather clothes and wellington boots; lengths of ribbon; string; gift-wrap tape.

THINK FIRST! Never leave your child unattended with lengths of ribbon or string.

Rainbow puddles

Sharing the game

- Help your child to get dressed to play out in the rain. Gently tie some lengths of ribbon to each of your hands and to your child's hands. Choose a length that will be sufficient to trail on the floor, but not enough to trip your child.
- Go outside with your child and trail the ribbons and lengths of string through the puddles to make trails. Look at the shapes that you are making. Use describing words and prompt your child to copy you. Talk about the length of the trails, and about the shapes and patterns that you make.
- Trail the ribbons slowly, and then quickly through the puddles. Look at the different patterns together. Encourage your child to use two- and three-word phrases, such as 'tiny drops', 'long, slithery snake' and so on.
- Stamp in the puddles, adding footprints to your trails. Count the footprints as you stamp. Then walk on your tiptoes or balance on your heels. Look together at the different shapes of your footprints. Make footprints next to each other and talk about big and little shapes.
- Give your child plenty of time to think about and explore the shapes as well as to talk and listen to you.

Taking it further

- Make alternating patterns with big and small footprints.
- Find some twigs, leaves and feathers to create trails.
- Roll some pebbles through the puddles and talk about the shapes that they make.

JUST THE TWO OF US

STAGE
Putting words together

LEARNING OPPORTUNITIES
- To play together, imitating actions
- To make a choice.

YOU WILL NEED
A length of stretchy fabric; two lengths of ribbon.

Slithery snake

Sharing the game

- Roll the fabric up to create a long snake shape. Tie each end securely with a ribbon.
- Sit on the floor. Hold one end of the snake and give the other end to your child to hold so that the snake is stretched out between you.
- Wriggle the snake from side to side on the floor. Say, 'Wriggle, wriggle, wriggle, stop!' and stop the snake abruptly.
- Ask your child if she would like the snake to move up and down. Say, 'Up, down, up, down, up, down, stop!' again stopping abruptly.
- Invite your child to choose what the snake should do next. Give her time to think about this without interruption. Use her suggestion, or offer a choice of the two actions that you have already used, such as 'Wriggle, wriggle or up and down?'.

- Play a game with each of you pulling the snake, then counting together, 'One, two, three', before letting go of the stretched-out snake. Play again, letting your child count, and let go of the snake.
- Coil the snake up and curl up next to it. Tell your child that the snake is tired. Encourage your child to curl up and copy your actions.
- Wake up the snake and ask your child what she thinks the snake will do next. Offer her a choice of the games that you have played with the snake. When your child has made her choice, play the game.
- Repeat your child's choice of game, this time asking her if the snake is going to do it slowly or really fast. Vary the pace of the game to match your child's response. Take it in turns to make the choices.

Taking it further

- Make two snakes, one long and one much shorter. Offer your child a choice of which snake to play each game with.
- Coil the snake up and look together at the spiral shape. Where else can you find spiral shapes? Draw or make spirals, for example, with spaghetti, or drawing spirals with wet fingers on a dry surface.

JUST THE TWO OF US

STAGE
Putting words together

LEARNING OPPORTUNITIES
- To use an object word and action word together
- To use plurals for more than one familiar object, such as 'books' or 'cars'.

YOU WILL NEED
Two hand puppets; small pile of bricks; shoebox containing toy cars; book; small blanket; cup; spoon.

Puppet play

Sharing the game

- Sit opposite your child and invite him to choose one of the puppets to hold. Place the other puppet on your hand and make it dance as you sing one of your child's favourite songs or rhymes.
- Make your puppet pick up the spoon and pass it to your child. Ask him if he would like to pretend to give the puppet some dinner. Then say, 'Look, (*puppet's name*) is eating. Do you want to give him a drink?'. Encourage your child to give your puppet a pretend drink from the cup.
- Let the puppet go to sleep on the blanket, and ask your child, 'Look, what is (*puppet's name*) doing?'. Prompt your child to respond with a two-word phrase, including an action word. Repeat, pretending to make the puppet jump, run, clap its hands and so on.
- Encourage your child to make his puppet copy the actions of your puppet. Ask your child what his puppet is doing.
- Next, make your puppet open the shoebox with the cars inside. Ask your child what is inside. Encourage him to use the plural form 'cars' rather than 'car'.
- Now let your puppet stack up the pile of bricks and encourage your child to describe what the puppet is doing. If your child uses one word, for example, 'bricks', reply by saying, 'Yes, (*puppet's name*) is building'.

Taking it further

- Give your child a puppet or soft toy to hold as you read a story to him. Help him to make the toy or puppet imitate some of the actions that he sees in the pictures or hears in the story.

JUST THE TWO OF US

STAGE
Putting words together

LEARNING OPPORTUNITIES
- To use some words to describe feelings
- To talk about past events.

YOU WILL NEED
Some card; coloured paper; sticky tape; photographs of your child and family members; photograph of your child as a baby; old catalogues and magazines; scissors; felt-tipped pens; glue.

All about me

Sharing the game

- Create a simple book containing approximately six blank pages.
- Help your child to glue a photograph of herself to the front cover of the book and to 'write' her name. Encourage her to decorate it by making marks and drawing pictures of family members, favourite toys or characters.
- Look at the family photographs together and encourage your child to talk about the different people.
- Glue the photographs into the book. Let your child add her own marks, and write your child's words next to each photograph.
- Add a baby photograph of your child to the book, and talk about when she was a baby. Help her to find pictures of baby items in the catalogues and magazines, such as a bib. Cut them out and glue them on to the page.
- Make similar pages combining photographs, drawings, your child's marks and your writing of her words. Create pages about grandparents, your child's bedroom, nursery, friends and so on.
- With each page, focus on words to describe feelings and emotions such as 'happy', 'sad', 'sleepy', 'angry' and so on. Listen carefully to your child, and write, using her own words, on each page.
- Look at the book together regularly and add extra pages, pictures or words, as your child wishes. Use it as a basis for talking and listening to your child about her feelings and for helping her to think about important events and people in her life.

Taking it further

- Add a handprint, or a lock of your child's hair, to the book. Encourage your child to collect and keep mementoes to add to the book, such as special birthday cards.

Ten tips for encouraging your child's language development

1 Share books and pictures with your baby and young child every day. Look at picture books, story-books, information books, poems and rhymes. Share pictures in magazines and focus on print and pictures as you go about your daily life together, such as at the shops, on the way to nursery and so on.

2 Make time for songs, finger rhymes and nursery rhymes, not only with your baby, but also with your child as she will learn a lot from songs and rhymes.

3 When sharing books and pictures with your baby, support her head well and hold the pictures close to her face. (A baby will focus best on objects held approximately 23cm from her face.)

4 Find a few minutes of uninterrupted, unhurried time each day to listen to your child.

5 When playing together, sit on the floor with your child, or kneel down next to her, so that your faces are at the same level.

6 Say your child's name before you speak, so that she is looking and listening.

7 Turn off the television and radio to minimise distractions as you play. Put some toys away so that sometimes your child is focused on just one or two toys.

8 Give your child every opportunity to look at pictures and print, and to make marks using crayons or pencils.

9 Enjoy music with your child, relax and have fun together. Try to minimise the amount of television that your child watches alone. Choose carefully what your child watches and, when appropriate, watch programmes together, talking about what you see and linking this into your child's world.

10 Try to tune into your baby and child's communication, what she understands and how she converses with you, for example, by sounds, looks, gestures, pointing or words. Enjoy playing together, but also allow plenty of time for your child to play independently.

USEFUL CONTACTS

AFASIC
2nd Floor, 50–52 Great Sutton Street, London EC1V 0DJ
Tel: 020-7490 9140, fax: 020-7251 2834
AFASIC helpline: 0845-355 5577
E-mail: info@afasic.org.uk
Visit the website: www.afasic.org.uk
An organisation that promotes understanding and support for children and young people with speech and language difficulties.

I CAN
4 Dyer's Buildings, Holborn, London EC1N 2QP
Tel: 0870-010 4066, fax: 0870-010 4067
Visit the website: www.ican.org.uk
A national educational charity for children with speech and language difficulties.

Booktrust
Book House, 45 East Hill, London SW18 2QZ
Tel: 020-8516 2984, fax: 020-8516 2978
Book information service: 0906-516 1193
An independent educational charity for advice and information about children's books, including 'Bookstart', a national 'books for babies' programme.

Are you worried about your child's language development?

Babies and young children all develop at different rates, although their learning usually follows the same path. Some babies make faster progress in certain areas of their development than others for a whole range of reasons, while other babies will have developed further in other areas.

Babies do not progress at a steady pace. They will have phases when they appear to make rapid progress with their language skills, and other times when they seem to be at the same stage for quite some time. This is not unusual and is a time when the child is busy making rapid development in other areas, perhaps with motor skills, for example, movement and handling objects. It can also be a time when your child is simply consolidating what he has recently learned and practising new skills.

However, if you do have any concerns about your child's language development, contact your health visitor or family doctor. Explain your concerns and check that your child has had a hearing assessment. Sometimes it is difficult to pinpoint your concerns. It can help to describe your child's language skills in terms of the following:

- How does your child let you know what he wants? Does he use gestures, pointing, words or glances? Does he pass you objects that he needs help with?
- Does your child understand familiar routines, know what is going to happen next, respond to his name, understand single words or know the names of familiar objects?
- What does your child like to do? Who does he like to play with? Does he have any particular likes or dislikes? When is your child most communicative?
- Does your child use words but is difficult to understand? Write down some of what he says, as he says it, and with the intended meaning next to it.

All this will help you to think clearly about your concerns and explain them more effectively, so that you can get the best help and attention for your child.